THE
WORK OF THE
CHURCH
TRUSTEE

THE
WORK OF THE
CHURCH
TRUSTEE

ORLANDO L. TIBBETTS

Judson Press ® Valley Forge

THE WORK OF THE CHURCH TRUSTEE

Copyright © 1979
Judson Press, Valley Forge, PA 19482-0851
Ninth Printing, 1991

Unless otherwise indicated, Bible quotations in this volume are from the *Good News Bible*—Old Testament: Copyright © American Bible Society 1976; New Testament: Copyright © American Bible Society 1966, 1971, 1976.

Other versions of the Bible quoted in this book are:

The Holy Bible, King James Version.

The Revised Standard Version of the Bible, copyrighted 1946, 1952, 1971, 1973 © by the Division of Christian Education of the National Council of the Churches of Christ in the United States of America, and are used by permission.

Library of Congress Cataloging in Publication Data

Tibbetts, Orlando L.
   The work of the church trustee.

   Includes bibliographical references.
   1. Church trustees.   I. Title.
BV705.T5   254   79-9882
ISBN 0-8170-0825-X

The name JUDSON PRESS is registered as a trademark in the U.S. Patent Office.
Printed in the U.S.A.

To William E. Braisted, M.D.,
Margaret A. Gardiner,
Sydney F. Fuller
for their being the kind of
Christian leaders I have written about
in this book.

Other books of interest:

Church Officers at Work (Revised)

Glenn H. Asquith

The Deacon at Work

Frederick A. Agar

Superintendents Plan Their Work (Revised)

Idris W. Jones

The Work of the Church Treasurer

Thomas E. McLeod

The Work of the Clerk (Revised)
Zelotes Grenell and Agnes Grenell Goss

The Work of the Deacon and Deaconess

Harold Nichols

The Work of the Usher

Alvin D. Johnson

Work of the Church: Getting the Job Done in Boards and Committees

David R. Sawyer

Work of the Pastoral Relations Committee

Emmett V. Johnson

Preface

In every author's mind is the thought of that special book which he or she would like to write. At the same time most authors have in mind the book they hope never to write. Well, this book happens to be the one I never hoped or expected to write. The reason for my not expecting to write this book was precisely because I had fallen into the trap, known to so many of us, of thinking the board of trustees was that group of business-types who handled the maintenance of the church—and no more!

But when I was asked by the Reverend Harold Twiss of Judson Press if I would consider writing a book for the boards of trustees in local churches, I began to give new thought and prayerful consideration to the challenge. I remembered my own hopes and dreams as a pastor; I remembered how I yearned for a board of trustees which accepted its responsibilities within the sacred purpose of Christ's holy will. And I'm happy to say I knew such people, and boards, and have drawn heavily from those experiences with appreciation to them.

As I became excited about this writing, I interviewed a

number of trustees and former trustees. I visited boards of trustees and sat in their meetings as an observer. I want to express my appreciation to the following for their help in personal interviews or board meetings: Mr. Frederick Burton of Lakewood, Ohio; Mrs. Florence Doutre of Saginaw, Michigan; Mr. Morgan Noyes of Groton, Connecticut; Mrs. Virginia Leukhardt of Waterbury, Connecticut; Mr. Al Shafer of South Windsor, Connecticut; Mr. Kenneth Case of Canton, Connecticut; and Mr. Walter Lawrence of Manchester, Connecticut.

In addition I want to thank the Reverend Alex Elsesser of East Longmeadow, Massachusetts, and the Reverend George Lang of Thompson, Connecticut, for their valuable technical and resource helps.

This book has been written to put into the hands of people who are being asked to serve on a board of trustees, or of those who are now serving and would like to deepen and widen their own sense of ministry and mission through the board. My hope is that it will be used as a stimulus and inspiration. It was written to underscore the biblical and theological basis of service. It was written with a personal, case study approach in order to help us realize that there are common concerns and needs which we face as members of trustee boards.

The case studies in chapter 8 are based upon authentic happenings and data, from actual boards of trustees' meetings. But the names, churches, places, etc., are changed in order to protect the people who were involved.

Finally, I want to extend a word of deep appreciation to Carol Freehan for typing this manuscript. As always, she has shown great patience and persistence in helping me with this tremendous task.

Orlando L. Tibbetts
Hartford, Connecticut

Contents

Chapters

Chapter 1

Who Make the Best Trustees?

Rachel was still in a state of shock! She had just been approached by a member of her church's nominating committee who asked if she would be willing to serve on the church's board of trustees. "Who? Me?" she had asked this well-meaning member of the nominating committee. "I'm not the kind of person you need for that board! You must be kidding! The missionary committee or the board of Christian education are places where I could serve best. But, the board of trustees; no way!" And with this response Rachel had shut the door on what she thought was a finished matter.

A few days later Rachel's minister dropped by her home to chat with her. He explained he was there because a disturbed member of the nominating committee had come to the conclusion that some people had a mistaken idea of what it means to serve as a trustee in a local church. Rachel and her pastor talked at great length about who should serve on a board of trustees, what were the qualifications, and was she the type of person they needed? The minister's concepts were different from what Rachel had always thought. She admitted that her stereotypes of trustees were prestigious men, who were bankers, lawyers, accountants, realtors, insurance agents, contractors, or experts in the world of business. She was none of these. Besides, if she gave her time anywhere in the church, it would be in some job that had a *spiritual purpose* which was far above that of a board of trustees!

Rachel's minister responded to her high standards and said, "That's exactly what I'm talking about! We need you to join with others as trustees of God's people, and God's church, to carry out God's will! We are not asking you to separate your faith from this job; nor are we asking you to become a part of something that is purely secular business as opposed to the sacred business. We need trustees in this church who realize they have been given a trust to hold and a task to do that is saturated with prayer and motivated by Christ's love." He assured her that there would be a new day in the church if people with her spiritual maturity and mission vision would put their lives on the line and serve as the "new breed of trustee."

What Is a Trustee, Anyway?

The concern of people like Rachel and her minister is not uncommon. Many people in the church are looking prayerfully and intelligently at the existing boards and committees. They are asking: "Who needs them? Where do they come from? Can we simplify the church structures and give more time to the essentials of the gospel?"

One of the most difficult boards in the church to define and understand is the board of trustees. This is because the church is a spiritual body which cannot be incorporated properly. So, a parallel body, or an internal body, becomes the legal entity before the state.

Dr. William Leach, in his *Toward a More Efficient Church,* tells us, "There are two common methods of church incorporation: 'Trustee Incorporation' and 'Membership Incorporation.' In the former, trustees are elected by the incorporated society to hold the property of the church. Once such an incorporation has been set up, it is perpetual until changes are made on application to the proper state agency."[1] This is one form of trusteeship, but there is also another.

In many churches the whole membership is the group of trustees before the state. But a special smaller number are elected as a board of trustees (or stewards) to care for the property of the church.

This usually means not only the buildings but also the total material possessions of the church are managed by the board of trustees. This is why churches have used the old practice of choosing people to serve on these boards who have business experience, financial know-how, and perhaps the banker's instincts.

Various dictionaries help us in defining the trustee by reminding us that trustees are persons "who manage for others," or "who hold title on behalf of others." The word "TRUST" is the key word. It means that a church has put its confidence in a group of its members and has given them the duty of caring for their material posessions.

[1] William H. Leach, *Toward a More Efficient Church* (New York: Fleming H. Revell Co., 1948), p. 43.

The Scriptural Basis for Trustees

As people of the Word we turn to the Scriptures to seek guidance in this matter of church trustees. Unfortunately we do not find the word "trustee" in the Bible, in the sense in which we use it today, except where we are all reminded of the fact that we are STEWARDS of all that God has given us. But we do have some teachings that are relevant for trustees.

In the sixth chapter of Acts we read a passage that is often used as the basis for a board of deacons. But, if we read it more carefully, we can see that there is not a very clear distinction between our concepts of deacons and trustees.

> Some time later, as the number of disciples kept growing, there was a quarrel between the Greek-speaking Jews and the native Jews. The Greek-speaking Jews claimed that their widows were being neglected in the daily distribution of funds. So the twelve apostles called the whole group of believers together and said, "It is not right for us to neglect the preaching of God's word in order to handle finances. So then, brothers, choose seven men among you who are known to be full of the Holy Spirit and wisdom, and we will put them in charge of this matter. We ourselves, then, will give our full time to prayer and the work of preaching."
>
> The whole group was pleased with the apostles' proposal, so they chose Stephen, a man full of faith and the Holy Spirit . . . (Acts 6:1-5).

The passage goes on to tell of the other men elected with Stephen.

Without getting into a biblical argument over whether these were deacons or trustees, the fact remains that they were given a task of caring for the management and distribution of funds, and that is a trusteeship! It is my contention that God never intended that financial matters, or the management of buildings, or the monitoring of fiscal matters, should be separated from the responsibilities that have "diakonia" or service as the very heart of all administration. Just as a deacon must be trusted with special funds and special spiritual concerns of the church, so the trustees must "deaconize" with a service-oriented administration of properties because they all serve the same Father God with the same missionizing purpose as found in Jesus Christ.

The Marks of a Member of the Board of Trustees

Beginning with what the church is all about, we would affirm that a church trustee should *be a person of the Word.* This does not mean that such a person has to be a Bible scholar, or even a walking Bible dictionary. But, surely he or she should have a general knowledge of the Word of God as it relates to the theology of the church and the reason why the church was established.

Sometimes, when we insist upon such a high standard for a member of the board of trustees, we frighten away people with tremendous potential for being leaders in the church. The Master gave us a clue to this. He chose people who were not founded and grounded in his Word, but who were open to learning the Word and its implications for them. That's why it is a good idea to have training sessions for church officers in the church. In a retreat time or series of training events a board of trustees, like all the other boards and committees, can then spend time beginning with questions, such as: Why did Jesus establish this church anyway? What are our roles as servants of his church and world? How do we relate the properties and possessions of the church to the whole question of Christian stewardship in the community and world?

There are stories in the Old Testament concerning the temple of God which have some relevance for trustees. But the New Testament has more yet. In Philippians we read: "Don't do anything from selfish ambition or from a cheap desire to boast; but be humble toward one another, always considering others better than yourselves. And look out for one another's interests, not just for your own" (Philippians 2:3-4). In 2 Corinthians 4:1, we read, "God in his mercy has given us this work to do, and so we do not become discouraged. We put aside all secret and shameful deeds; we do not act with deceit, nor do we falsify the word of God. In the full light of truth we live in God's sight and try to commend ourselves to everyone's good conscience."

These are just a few of the Scriptures we can contemplate as we consider the marks of a church trustee. But the most important words were spoken by Jesus when he said, "My commandment is this: love one another, just as I love you. The greatest love a person can have for his friends is to give his life for them. And you are my friends if you do what I command you. I do not call you servants any longer, because a servant does not know what his master is doing. Instead, I call you friends, because I have told you everything I heard from my Father. You did not choose me; I chose you and appointed you to go and bear much fruit, the kind of fruit that endures" (John 15:12-16).

So, remembering as Christian church trustees that our call

to serve is to be stamped with his word and filled with his Spirit, we enter this responsibility with humility and sincerity. As "branches" on his vine (John 15:1-4), we will be guided by his Word and will.

The second mark of a church trustee is *spiritual sensitivity*. By this I mean that whoever serves on a board of trustees should *be a person who loves the church* and is sensitive to its needs. Here we are not speaking of the church as some static institution built upon a history of superficial traditions. Instead, we mean the church as the gathered people who have a common faith in Jesus Christ as the Lord of all of life. This means then that everything which happens in that board meeting is taking place within the framework of ministry and mission. Not all church officers understand what is meant by this—especially, boards of trustees. All too many trustees feel their responsibility is to perpetuate a building, maintain edifices, monitor fiscal matters, and have a good balance in the bank book. For the spiritually sensitive trustee, there is always in mind the question, what is the will of God in these matters? Furthermore, the spiritually sensitive will also ask: "How does the maintenance or improvement of this building better enhance the proclaiming of the gospel? When do you make decisions because it's God's will for the church even though the decisions are not based upon sound business principles?" In fact, some of the most exciting churches in this land were led to decide on a deficit budget, or an expenditure which didn't make business sense, but was the will of the people in faith.

Sometimes a board of trustees may decide out of a sense of Christian social responsibility to give up an investment, or lose a profit, because it's the only way for God's church to witness in a world of injustice and inequality.

The third mark of a member of the board of trustees should be that of *teamwork capabilities*. This concept of teamwork means two things: the trustee functions as a member of the larger team, the CHURCH, and thus is always responsible to them; and secondly the trustee is one of a number of trustees and should know how to work with a small group of people without having to dominate them.

A team person learns to listen and to be sensitive to other opinions. A team person volunteers to pick up his or her share of the labors and make the load lighter for all. A strong board of trustees may have every type and kind of individual, but it's only as each accepts the unique task of which he or she is capable that the board can function effectively.

The fourth mark of a member of the board of trustees is *openness*. This group is given a great responsibility in overseeing the physical buildings and possibly the financial affairs of the whole church. (Some churches do have separate finance boards or committees.) This means, then, they must be open to change, flexible in opinions, and willing to learn.

Many churches have had great problems because members of their board of trustees were only interested in the building and its care. This meant that if a board of Christian education wanted a decision made to alter a room, increase a budget item, or to open the building for community use, it was blocked by a group of hard-dealing business types who couldn't see that board's purpose and then prevented the changes from being made.

Openness will be more of a characteristic of trustee board members if more of them have served on mission committees, social concern committees, Christian education boards, or music committees where they have had a previous orientation to concerns which result in openness.

Finally, one of the marks of a member of the board of trustees *ought to be some skills in property and financial matters.* A trustee ought to be a person of impeccable character, innate honesty, and the ability to use good judgment in property and financial decision making. It does not always follow that the best trustees are from the business world. Yet if a church can find a business-world person who has all the other marks suggested, all the better. You do need people who understand property deeds, stock transfers, mortgages, and bank notes. You will also find people valuable who understand heating systems and electrical wiring. But every board should be balanced with some wiser men and women who are quick to learn and sensitive in other directions. In other words, be sure, in your church, that your board has skilled people on it who care for people as well as property; and you will have a strong board of trustees.

One further word should be said about having young people on the board of trustees. Even though the younger people on the board will not have had the experience with the management of properties or funds, they do have the same responsibility toward those areas of the church life as do the older members of the gathered church. It's not a question of the young being the church of tomorrow; they are already the church of today. So, membership of youth on a board of trustees recognizes their part in the shared trust of the church and also brings into focus a viewpoint which every board needs.

Finding the Right Persons to Serve as Trustees

Every church should have a bylaw description of what a trustee does. But it's very likely that every church will not have a description of the kind of person who ought to serve on the board. In the previous pages we have already given some "Marks of a Member of a Board of Trustees." These are really the setting up of ideals toward which to aim. But what is the process we use to find such persons?

Unfortunately, too many nominating committees take the shortcut by begging anyone to fill a job that needs to be done whether or not he or she is qualified to take on the responsibility that is being required.

Every church should prepare a list of "marks desired" for all its officers. Then, putting these together with simple job descriptions, they should seek out, prayerfully, those individuals who will best fill those offices. Notice that we said *prayerfully!* The head and the heart of a nominating committee should be fully committed to Jesus Christ and his purposes for his church. Even as the apostle Paul wrote to the early Christians and said, "Let this mind [of Christ] be in you," so a group of people who choose and nominate another group of people to take upon them the trust which Jesus has left to us has an awesome responsibility. It must be undergirded with more than perfunctory prayer.

In the nominating committee meeting the group should ask, "Who are the people in our church who have the 'marks' we are seeking and who have a holistic view of the church?

How can we get a sure balance of business-world skills and spiritual compassion? How can we get the right balance of financial understandings and dedication to mission?" Seek out persons who know the ministry side of your church as well as the management styles of your community. Then, after much prayer, go to them with a frank challenge to sacrifice and commitment. Too many people who never felt a call to true servanthood have been elected to boards, and thus they were unable to give of their best to their task.

The Decision Made

Let's return now to Rachel and her problem with the invitation which came to become a candidate before the church as a potential member of the board of trustees. Her conversations with her pastor, coupled with her prayer talks with God, led her to the conclusion that the cross would have no meaning for her unless she was willing to say, "Here am I, Lord; use me."

As she reflected upon the deeper meaning of trusteeship, she realized that not only had God placed this world and its resources in our hands, but he had also placed the church and its resources in his followers' hands. Since these are God's, made more wonderful through Christ's gift of his life, she had an obligation to give the best she had as a trustee of grace. Rachel realized she didn't have a great deal of expertise in management of corporation resources, but she did manage her own finances, and she had property for which she had been responsible. But most of all, she loved the Lord, she loved his people, she loved the church, and she had a burning desire to give her life in such a way that people would learn to trust God and each other. So, trusteeship took on a new meaning to Rachel as she said, "yes," with a mixture of fear and faith. She had discovered that the gap is not all that great between being the keeper of the keys of the church and keeper of the keys to the kingdom.

Questions to Ponder or Discuss

1. Have you ever felt the way Rachel did about the qualifications for being a trustee?
2. Are there other "marks" that you would add to the list of "dream qualifications"?
3. What do you consider to be a "holistic view" of the church, and how does this affect the functioning of a board of trustees?

Chapter 2

It's a Big Job

The state conference on "Training Church Leaders" was now being told by the presiding chairperson where the various workshops would be held. Several hundred laypersons had come from various churches throughout the state.

Nathaniel Williams was excited about being there. He had just been elected to the board of trustees of his church and it was a first for him. He had spent a number of years on the board of deacons, but being a trustee was a whole new challenge! He supposed that the nominating committee had presented his name because he had recently been named vice-president at the bank. True, he thought, as he entered the workshop room with the others, he was at home with figures and finances, but something told him his job was much more than that.

The workshop leader introduced himself and then suggested that each person in the group say something about the church from which he or she came and what expectations he or she might have for this all-day session.

It was interesting for Nathaniel to hear that at least half of those present had never served on a board of trustees before. They were as overwhelmed by the prospect as he was. One woman said her board was called a board of stewards. He liked that term; it said something special to him. The rest of those present were the "pros." Some had served off and on for many years and had come to this particular workshop to see if they could find solutions to some of the frustrating problems they faced as trustees.

Nathaniel noticed that there were some other blacks present, and he wondered if his church and theirs had any peculiar problems that a white leader couldn't address. Well, he'd just have to see. He remembered that being a deacon in his church was very different from the experiences of his white friends, but as a trustee, he couldn't believe there were any differences.

Using newsprint and a Magic Marker, the leader proceeded to tell the group that he was building his entire approach for the day around the 4M factor. Banker Williams became a student once again and began to take notes.

The Trustees as Managers (the first "M")

It is possible that there are those in the church who believe that the word "management" is foreign to the ongoing work of the local church. They have no trouble associating it with a bank or factory or school or store, but not the church. After all, we are the spiritual body of the Lord!

If one reads the Bible carefully, it will be discovered that from its earliest pages the question of management and administration is lifted up before God's people. Good church management originates in the Old Testament where the children of God are guided toward strong administrative principles in order more effectively to carry the purposes of God through his people into the world.

There is an intriguing account in Exodus 11 concerning the children of Israel wandering through the wilderness of Sinai under the leadership of the great leader Moses. In a real sense this was the beginning of the model for the church to come. At its center was the worship of Yahweh God, the teaching of God's people, and the fulfillment of the establishment of God's kingdom on earth.

A relatively unknown person entered the picture. His name was Jethro, and we hear of him in a previous account in Exodus 3 which describes the time Moses as a young unemployed person worked for him as a shepherd and eventually married Jethro's daughter, Zipporah.

As we read Exodus, chapter 18, we discover that this Jethro, a priest of Midian, and father-in-law of the now great conqueror and leader of the Israelites, made a journey into the wilderness and eventually discovered the whereabouts of his son-in-law. Not being content to talk platitudes and to share news from back home, he took Moses into a tent and said, "You're doing it all wrong! As an administrator of the tribes you're killing yourself by not managing the people effectively." Then he proceeded to instruct Moses on good management. The story, for our purposes, says the following:

1. Good tribal (church) management requires openness to new ideas and ways. (Exodus 18:24)

2. Good tribal (church) management requires the full utilization of all the leaders available. (Exodus 18:21-23)

3. Good tribal (church) management attempts to lead people to action as well as decisions. (Exodus 18:14)

4. Good tribal (church) management requires good organization. Like the Hebrew tribes of old the church of today is not a single-celled unit which can be managed simplistically. It is complex, composed of program and buildings, people and purpose. (Exodus 18:17-18)

5. Good tribal (church) management has worship and spiritual growth as its motivating power. (Exodus 18:12)

The board of trustees, with the pastor and deacons, are the comanagers of these internal aspects of the life of the church which relate to finances and physical properties. They keep a recording of all details related to these and seek ways to carry out the purposes of the church through proper administrative procedures. They are a management team, under the leadership of the pastor, who is the general manager.

Ever keeping in mind that they are the servants of the church who are charged with the responsibilities of budget control, the trustees have two major concerns. The first concern is whether there will be money enough to carry out the voted mandates of the membership; they must also make certain that the money is spent according to the will of the people. As good managers, they will resist the temptation of all trustees to determine ways of budget control which mitigate against a sense of family within the church. The control factors should have been made clear in a well-developed budget, but there should always be flexibility and consultation. The highest types of trustees do not consider themselves the sole authorities in final decision making. When there is a matter impinging upon the work of the board of Christian education or diaconate or missions committee, the chairperson, in consultation with the minister and the heads of those boards or committees, should seek full, two-way communication.

Some boards of trustees have full responsibility for the control of the use of the properties. Here again, the board should not set itself apart as an isolated group of decision makers who determine how and when the buildings should be used. Instead, the board is the managing unit which carries out the wishes of the whole church membership. If the church body, for example, decides that the Parents without Partners group may use the social hall every Tuesday evening, then the board of trustees has the responsibility to honor that decision. Its task is to see that the building is ready for use; that the group is given a key, or that the custodian or a member of the board is on hand to open the doors. If time proves that this was not a wise decision, then the chairperson of the trustees should communicate this to the governing body of the church. In that democratic forum a decision can be made as to whether or not this group should continue to have access to the social hall.

If the church decides to remodel a building, or purchase parking facilities, or expand its edifice, it may move to seek a loan from a loaning institution. The board of trustees would be the group that does all the negotiating and signing of documents. It would act on behalf of the church making certain all legal technicalities are properly considered.

Finally, as managers of the church's fiscal affairs, the board of trustees should always be keenly sensitive to the future needs of the congregation. They should join with the other boards and committees of the church in projecting needs over a five-, ten-, or twenty-year period of time. Together the key leaders of the church should do occasional dreaming about the direction the community is going, the need for changes within the church, and the desirability of changing the shape of the ministry and mission of that church. This may require an inventory by the board of trustees of the present budget, the present buildings, and the present locale around the church property. Out of this can come suggestions for change. They could even suggest a redistribution of space needs, or a reduction of such needs. Then again, they may help the church to expand its facilities in order to have a more adequate ministry in that location. Sometimes a board of trustees helps its members to see that the present facilities can no longer be utilized as a form of good stewardship and should be completely demolished and rebuilt, or perhaps the church should seek to move elsewhere. Good managers never take the status quo position.

The Trustees as Maintenance Supervisors (the second "M")

Unless the bylaws of the church designate the responsibility otherwise, the board of trustees has the full responsibility for the care and maintenance of the church buildings. This would include parsonages, or manses, and any other buildings which the church may own. Some churches have a subcommittee under their board of trustees which is called a Properties Committee or a House Committee. It oversees the general use of the building's rooms, in cooperation with the other boards and committees. It may develop an "assignment chart" so that the various groups will not run into a conflict of space and time.

We have already mentioned the board of trustees' responsibility in managing the usage of the church by "outside" groups. This will also require maintenance decisions. Who will clean areas before and after they are used? Who will set the cost figure to cover this? Because the church is a nonprofit, tax-exempt facility which is for community usage, any compensation should be used strictly to cover the extra costs. This should be determined by the board of trustees. An arrangement should be made to enable proper covering of those maintenance costs of cleaning, wear and tear, and the use of utilities.

The maintenance of the church buildings is a very responsible and time-consuming task. Though a church may have a custodian or assistants who take care of the small problems like repairing a leaky faucet or replacing defective light bulbs, he or she should not be responsible for making major repairs or alterations. When there is a flooding of the basement, caused by a faulty roof gutter, or a serious furnace problem that jeopardizes the whole heating system, then it is important for the board of trustees to make major decisions that will remedy the problems.

Each board of trustees (or Property Committee) ought to establish a timetable and checklist for properly determining needs which may arise in the maintenance of the church buildings. Too often churches respond to emergencies as they arise, rather than have a continuous and thorough means of determining needs.

As a board begins its new year with new members added, there should be a forward look to the needs which might arise during the year and a planned process by which those needs might be anticipated.

A good leader and chairperson will then assign responsibilities to various individuals for constant monitoring. If an electrician is on the board, then it would be natural to appoint him or her to check out the wiring systems and adequacies of the electrical systems within the various buildings. This might make a difference in costs of insurance or in safety of life.

The Maintenance Checklist (Appendix A) is only an example of the kind of checklist which might be drawn up by a board. What is in that list will be determined by the kind and number of buildings you have or even by the number who might serve on your board or committee.

The Trustees in Ministry (the third "M")

In the Old Testament we read of the sons of Kohath, who were responsible for the furniture of the temple (see Numbers 4:1-15). In a very real sense the persons responsible for the care and maintenance of the church building are sons and daughters of Kohath who are providing the means for people to be ministered unto and to become ministers to others. The New Testament concept of the priesthood of believers only becomes a reality as we gather in the meeting place as members of the body of Jesus Christ.

Some trustees have no difficulty in seeing themselves as managers and maintenance people, but all too often they are not reminded that their special responsibilities involve them in ministry. So, the minister of the church will proclaim the Good News from the pulpit and teach the biblical concepts which enable people to be ministers to one another. But, the cleanliness of that sanctuary, the condition of those pews, the functioning of those lights, the temperature of the building—all contribute to make ministry possible. The eyes, ears, and souls of the people gathering in that church can be opened or closed according to the functioning of the board of trustees. This is a spiritual trust which has been given to this group of people in order to provide a means for God to become real in our lives. That's why prayer and theological contemplation are as important for trustees as they are for the deacons, elders, boards of Christian education, or any other group within the church.

The Trustees in Mission (the fourth "M")

The buildings of the local church are placed where they are, at a point in history, in order that the people of God may gather to study God's Word and discover the theological truths which will help to answer the questions which have arisen out of their struggle in life. In worship the church discovers breath for its body; in worship the church receives its marching orders for involvement in mission to the community and world.

If the church does not become that dynamic center for reconciliation through Jesus Christ, it is a "white-washed tomb" with nothing but putrid bodies within. If, however, the church becomes that place from which its members penetrate the community and world with the reconciling love of Jesus Christ, then it becomes what God intended it to be.

At the same time the church building becomes that place where the alienated, unloved, lonely, unwanted, and burdened people come to seek fellowship and release from what captivates them. The very approach to the church grounds gives out a message. If the parking facilities are adequate, the signs are properly displayed, the stairs are easy to manage, and the facilities are pleasant to the eyes, the outsider is being reached by the caring of the trustees with a mission.

Every board of trustees should do a very thorough check-up of its exterior and interior to ask whether they are adequate expressions of God's love and reach to people.

The same God who so loved that he gave his Son also gave this church to service the community. Then why shouldn't trustees spend time asking, with other church members, whether the church is a mission center to those around or a memorial to those who have passed on? The exciting board of trustees will be that which always keeps the biblical and theological "raison d'être" and constantly seeks to look at its buildings in terms of mission to others.

It's a Big Job!

On the way home from the workshop for trustees, Nathaniel Williams kept thinking of the four "M"s that the leader had written on the newsprint. He had to admit that this was a more holistic approach to trusteeship than he had thought. In checking himself he confessed he would have stopped after "management and maintenance," but the thoughts of ministry and mission appealed to him. Even as a banker caught up in the intricacies of the everyday economic world, he wanted more than anything else to serve his church as a banker who loved the Lord and had a concern for people. He was glad that being a trustee meant he was still serving with diakonia! The day had been worthwhile.

Questions to Ponder or Discuss

1. How do you react to the concept of trustees as managers?
2. Are there any maintenance items from your experience that are not in the "Maintenance Checklist for Church Buildings" found in the Appendix?
3. For a few moments, discuss with someone else your thoughts concerning the ministry and mission of trustees.

Chapter 3

Your Board Should Be
the Best

The moderator of the Church Council announced that he had one more item to present before he adjourned the meeting. With deliberate hesitation he took a letter from an envelope, adjusted his glasses nervously, and began to read:

To the Members of the Church Council at Trinity Church

Dear Friends:

I am writing this letter with some reluctance and no little measure of guilt, because I have loved my church through the years and have always given myself to serve wherever I've been asked.

Six months ago you elected me to serve as a member of the Board of Trustees. I entered into this new task with enthusiasm and willingness to work, even though my specialized work at the hospital leaves me little time for such involvement.

When I first began attending the Trustee Board meetings, I found one or two persons taking to themselves every responsibility. Our job seemed to be rubber-stamping decisions, which had already been made in between

37

meetings. After a few meetings I discovered I was bored to death and feeling quite useless. Finally, I came to the conclusion that this Board didn't need me; I could serve more effectively elsewhere. So—please accept my resignation. If you ever get this Board of Trustees running the way it should, then I may come back. But, for now I want to give my time to something where everyone is working.

Most sincerely,
Robert Hargraves, M.D.

A stunned silence fell over the council; the chairperson of the board of trustees felt that all eyes were upon him. Then he spoke: "This is somewhat embarrassing; Dr. Hargraves is a wonderful man, with many skills. I really had no idea he felt underutilized, or bored. In fact I was pleased he was asked to be on our board. I guess this tells me we've got to take a new look at how we function as a board."

The Introduction to the Board of Trustees

The above account of the resignation of Dr. Hargraves from the board of trustees actually happened (with the names changed, or course), and it leads us to a consideration of how a new member of a board is introduced to the board's purpose and responsibilities.

At the first meeting of the board, the first impressions are being made upon new members. Those who have served before and are coming back to continue for another term or two should be very sensitive to the newly elected members. The chairperson should likewise be sensitive to the need for creating an open, friendly atmosphere of interpersonal relationships. Together, the chairperson and continuing members should make an effort to enable the new members to feel welcome, and especially to feel needed.

The meeting should begin with a tone-setting experience of prayer and perhaps a devotional thought which creates a mood of spiritual motivation for trusteeship.

Next, each member should be introduced and asked to give some personal word about his or her expectations as a member of the board.

Then, the chairperson should take a few moments for orientation concerning the scope of responsibility of the board. Even those who have served previously need to be reminded once again of what they have taken upon themselves as a form of commitment to Christ's church. It should be made very clear how often the board meets. At this point the group may wish to agree upon a regular meeting day, i.e., the first Tuesday of each month.

One very important factor in an introductory meeting is to agree on the style of operation. For example, will members contact the chairperson and give agenda items before the meeting is held? Or will the board be divided into subcommittees, such as "grounds keeping," "housekeeping," "room assignments," "approval of bills" "insurance check-ing," "stewardship program," "parsonage," etc.? If the board is small, it may be possible for each person to take on one area of responsibility with freedom to co-opt other nontrustees to help carry out the necessary work.

At this meeting a secretary should be named, and it should be made clear that all aspects of discussion, decisions, and actions should be thoroughly recorded and kept in an accessible file drawer in the church office. If the trustees do not have such a drawer, obtaining one may well be their first action. It is always good to have a special folder for each member. Then these can be collected and kept in that same file drawer. The secretary should develop the habit of passing on to the church pertinent information concerning actions taken. This may happen through a brief paragraph in the church bulletin or through a formal report to the church council.

The chairperson should lay down ground rules for how the meetings will be handled. Each may agree that motions are not necessary, but that consensus will be recorded. It should be emphasized that every member should feel free to participate verbally; but all discussions should be routed through the chairperson, and only one discussion should be in progress at any one time.

It is always good for a board to have a clear indication of time frames. For example, if the meeting begins at 7:00 P.M., all should agree that it should end by 9:00 P.M. Advance preparation of the agenda can help a chairperson to plan so that one item will not take an hour at the beginning of the evening and other items are left unattended. Usually, if there is an understanding about a meeting beginning on time and ending at a specific time, members will feel more comfortable and there will be less attrition. Each person should be urged to be present on time and to remain until the agreed-upon adjournment.

The Duties of the Chairperson

Usually someone is named the chairperson by the church

body or at an organizational meeting because he or she has certain basic qualifications. It would be ideal for this person to have all of the 4 "M" factors of skills and concerns in management, maintenance, ministry, and mission, but not everyone can combine all these qualities within oneself. Regardless, the ideal person would be one with an ability to lead, a capacity to understand the intricacies of the trustee's life, and the spiritual sensitivity to those higher and more meaningful purposes of the church. It should be a person who can work with the minister and who knows how to work well with other people. A dictatorial type cannot make an effective board chairperson. The chairperson should be one who indicates through regular worship and through faithful stewardship a love for the church.

The chairperson should understand very clearly what are his or her duties and the purposes for which the board of trustees has been established. He or she should consult regularly with the minister and the moderator or president of the church body.

Before a meeting takes place, the chairperson should plan an agenda which could be duplicated for each member of the board. Time should also be allowed in that agenda for items to be brought up at the meeting.

The chairperson should arrive a few minutes early, making sure the church is unlocked, and arranging the meeting room so that it is pleasant, comfortable, and makes for a feeling of unity and friendliness. Today more and more groups are holding such meetings in their homes in order to economize on fuel.

After the meeting has been opened with a prayer seeking

God's will, the leader shares the agenda, calls for referral to the minutes of the previous meeting for updating, and then says a word about his or her goals for that evening. Every so often there should be occasional summaries of what is taking place and assignments to others who have expressed a willingness to carry them out.

Jobs should be distributed on the basis of interest, ability, and willingness to carry them out. For example, if the matter is insurance and the thought is expressed that someone should do some shopping around to see if more competitive prices and benefits can be secured, the chairperson should encourage Mrs. Smith, who has indicated some interest and expertise in insurance, to take on the assignment. Then, before the next meeting the chairperson should phone her to see if she has a report to make.

A good meeting will be guided by a firm person who insists that members stay on the topic under discussion until it has been thoroughly disposed of by referral or by action.

Finally, the chairperson should constantly remind the board members that they are responsible to the parent body. Not all actions can be taken by the board. They must come back to the church for major actions.

Effectiveness Checklist—Board of Trustees

Your chairperson and members of the board of trustees may find it helpful to use the following checklist as a means of asking questions regarding the board's feelings about function and effectiveness. There may be other items which your trustees would add in order to have some form of evaluation.

Yes	Some-what	Not at all	
			We consider ourselves ministers of God in a spiritual task.
			We seek God's will at all meetings.
			We have regular meetings.
			Regular records are kept.
			Reports are made to the church membership.
			All members participate in discussions.
			Tasks are assumed by all members.
			Members are on time and regular in attendance.
			A complete survey has been made of church needs.
			Regular reports of income and expenses are given.
			There is a strong mission concern.
			Attempts are made to beautify the property.
			The minister and boards are in constant communication.
			Long-range planning is going on.
			We have a sense of accomplishment.

The Stewardship of Board Members

Had Dr. Hargraves been on a board where he had felt some preparation had gone on before the meetings, or that he and the other members were being good stewards of their time and talent during the meetings, he would not have resigned. Too many good people are underutilized and hence are either bored or frustrated. The way a meeting is planned, prepared for, and conducted communicates both the seriousness and the vitality of the board's existence.

We can hope that the church which lost this valuable man's involvement at the trustee level also gained some new awareness of how best to involve its members. If the board member sees clearly the board's purpose and tasks, if the board has pleasant meetings that make one feel he or she is about the Father's business, if the chairperson has done the homework necessary in preparation for the meeting, and if the person on the board feels necessary and involved in true accomplishments, then he or she will stick with it and carry out the commitment to serve.

Questions to Ponder or Discuss

1. Make a list of what you consider to be five basic qualifications that a chairperson of a board of trustees should meet.
2. If you were Dr. Hargraves, how would you have handled his concern?
3. What special area of responsibility would you be willing to assume on the board of trustees?

Chapter 4

The Money in Your Hand

The group was enjoying itself at the denominational retreat center. The whole church board had come for two days of orientation, planning, and praying.

As far as Marie was concerned, she felt she needed prayer more than anything else! After all, she was a new member of the board of trustees, having been elected at the January annual meeting. Up until now she had pretty well managed to avoid being elected to an official board, but Jim Springer's sales pitch included the need of qualified women on the trustees' board and that did it.

In her present position at the insurance company she had attained an executive position with men and women of importance, and she wasn't about to have it any different in the church she loved. So, she had said, "Yes," and had looked forward to this retreat that brought the experienced and inexperienced together.

After a worship time led by the minister, the moderator of the church explained the purpose for their being together. He reminded them of the bylaw definitions of each board present, and that they were all part of the same family, working together for the same purposes. He stressed the spiritual foundations of the church and asked them to meet in separate rooms, as individual boards. Each group was to begin its meeting with silent reflection and imagine that Jesus Christ was present to chair that meeting! He asked them to think of the words, "Lo, I am with you always," and to keep those words in mind as they sought the Father's will.

Marie wasn't too sure how trustees could keep the Master in mind as they dealt with buildings and budget, but she thought it a challenge to try.

At the board of trustees' meeting the chairperson picked up on the moderator's suggestions and then proceeded to remind the members of the scope of their responsibilities. After questions and answers he proceeded to assign the people present to subcommittees with specific tasks. Some were put on the House Committee; some were assigned to the Grounds Committee, others to the Stewardship Committee; and Marie was placed on the Finance Committee. She was entering on a path that she had not walked before.

In some churches a finance committee is formed that is separate from the board of trustees, but in most churches the committee is an internal part of the board. The reason is that the finance committee is responsible for planning, overseeing, controlling, and coordinating the financial operations of the church. To separate the management, maintenance, mission, and ministry of the church from the financial umbrella of the total church is difficult. Hence a unified body of trustees who work and communicate with each other, regardless of how they are titled, is imperative.

The New Jargon

Not everyone who serves on a board of trustees or a finance committee is familiar with the jargon that is used, even though they may be executives like Marie. So, words like "assets," "liabilities," "posting," and "trial balance" join expressions like "liquid assets," "capital gains," and "zero budgeting" to boggle the mind. In fact, treasurers will often use different words and different systems, but the difference is all at the word level. Basically, accounting procedures are the same. It's just a matter of adapting one's mind and vocabulary to the system at hand.

Loudell O. Ellis, professor of accounting at the University of Alabama in Birmingham, has written an excellent book entitled *Church Treasurer's Handbook* (Judson Press, Valley Forge, 1978), which should be read by every trustee who has responsibility for church finances or by finance committee members who may want to sit at the feet of an accounting expert. Even though it may appear to be very technical, and in spite of the fact that it was written for church treasurers, it still is something that other people with financial responsibilities should read. It will help folk like Marie to be more comfortable in the budget and accounting world.

The System in Which You Work

The board of trustees, or the finance committee related to it as a subcommittee or peer board, has the burden upon it to manage the monies of the congregation responsibly. This means, as church managers, that there will be proper control and open accountability.

Ellis, in her *Church Treasurer's Handbook,* quotes *Management Accounting:*

> Churches accept and disburse millions of dollars in contributions but the management of these funds often is done by volunteers . . . on a part-time basis. Many have little experience in the field and their tenure is rarely long enough for them to gain proficiency. As a result, "muddling through" sometimes turns out to be the best description of churches' handling of their financial records.[1]

For those who have church money in their hands it is important to communicate the information concerning the handling of that money to the donors. The budget is one major tool which does this.

The purpose of a church budget is to provide a means for its dream to be set down with price tags attached. Aspirations, desires, and goals of the membership become a reality through the figures that are agreed upon for fulfilling the dream.

The budget is used as a measurement tool. It is used daily, weekly, and monthly to enable the trustees (or financial managers) to control expenditures. Improperly managed churches might wait until the end of a year to detect a problem area of overspending. But, frequent accountability sessions which have properly prepared accounting systems will prevent this from happening.

The budget as a measurement tool also helps the church to be reminded of its dream and in addition to evaluate the

[1] "Today's Sermon: Financial Management of Church Affairs," *Management Accounting* (December, 1972), p. 60, quoted by Loudell Ellis, *Church Treasurer's Handbook* (Valley Forge: Judson Press, 1978), p. 7.

actual fulfillment of that projected dream.

Many boards of trustees have full authority for budget control. This means that they give approval to the payment of bills according to the budget voted by the membership and according to the monies then available.

A simple, systematic form should be used by the treasurer who ought to work closely with the trustees. The following is an example of the kind of budget form which might be used:

January 1—June 30

Item	Budget for Year	Allowance to Date	Monthly Expenditure	Spent to Date	(Over)/ Under to Date
Pastor's Salary	$15,000	$7,250	$1,250	$7,250	—
Office Supplies	500	250	50	100	$150
Insurance	600	300	—	400	($100)

This kind of report helps to give information, to generate discussion, and to reveal those areas that are without problems and those which have them. For example, why was the insurance payment higher by this date? Is it higher because it's that time of year when a larger amount has to be paid out and everything will even out before the fiscal year is over? With the increase today in the cost of office supplies, will the $500 that was budgeted be adequate for the full year? Suppose there was $500 budgeted for work with the elderly, and only $10 had been spent from that area. Would this reflect a weakness in a department not carrying out the wishes of the church? Did someone neglect to remember a part of the outreach dream for the elderly? Should there be discussions with the department, or the deacons, or the church council?

The spending, or lack of spending, money may not get the church's work done, but it can serve to call attention to an idea which reflects a church's concerns and desires. Focusing attention on a budget may serve to return a church's attention to its original dream.

Another aspect of budget control is to keep in mind the seasonal cycles of the year. For example, as related to the maintenance of the church building, the utility bills will vary according to the time of the year. High utility expenditures will reflect the winter cold, but low utility expenditures in the winter months may indicate that certain bills are not being paid on time. Good trustees will manage to know the answers to variables in budgets, whether caused by weather or a slow-working treasurer.

This leads me to emphasize again the need for a treasurer's working closely with the board of trustees or a finance committee. My research shows that more often than not the treasurer works independently of the board and usually never meets with it. It is precisely for the need of budget control interpretation that it seems imperative that there be close communication between a treasurer and that body responsible as overseers of the church's assets. Since the treasurer is that person who safeguards the financial assets and is responsible for reporting on them, it seems best to have this team working closely through more than some pages of an accounting book.

It is the task of the board of trustees to control the budget expenditures, and this is often a source of conflict. Many people who do not know how the trustees function or why they took certain actions will look upon their decisions as being motivated by personal frugality rather than by the best interests of the church. Thus, we can see the greater need for communication. The trustees have been entrusted with money from others and should keep in mind at all times their responsibility to those persons.

If there is a shortage of funds, it is not the right of the trustees to balance the operating budget by borrowing from other funds for which it is responsible without specific authorization from the church council, or the church. To pay the minister's salary out of mission funds or the building fund may seem to be good business to some, but it actually hides from the congregation the serious nature of a financial crisis. They have a right to be informed of the negatives as well as the positives. It might be far better to borrow from a bank and thus allow the church more time to deal with the crisis. Most congregations will rise to the occasion if they are given all the facts and challenged to increase their giving.

Some boards of trustees have been given the task of raising all the money which comes into a church. More will be said about this in a later chapter. But for now it will be sufficient to say that there should always be a prayerful monitoring of the cash flow as an indicator of the spiritual health of the membership. Monitoring of the cash flow also helps to point up implications for the coming year or years. The cash flow in the life of a church is as crucial to the church's future planning as the blood pressure of a patient in a doctor's office is crucial to his or her future life plan. Even as the patient has to alter life-styles according to the diagnosis, so the church may have to alter its style. These alterations do not necessarily need to include a reduction of the budget; they could include an increase and an advance toward the fulfillment of more daring dreams.

Stretching the Church Dollars

There are all kinds of stories about church treasurers and trustees who have to stretch dollars. One such story is about the little, weakling-type man who accepted the challenge of the circus strong man to squeeze a drop out of the already squeezed-dry lemon. The drop came, and the surprised strong man asked what this weak-looking Casper Milque-toast person did. He responded, "I'm the church treasurer."

The treasurer and the board of trustees (or finance committee) have the unenviable task of making dollars stretch in an era of rapidly increasing inflation.

A well-working, concerned board will seek ways to stretch those dollars because that is good Christian stewardship. The following are just some suggestions of how to do this:

1. Centralize all your purchasing by having one person purchase for all areas of church life.

2. Utilize some central agency for purchasing, perhaps your state denominational headquarters will help you, i.e., for purchasing mimeograph paper.

3. Use your tax free number at all times.

4. Make special efforts to utilize people in your church who will volunteer services to do plumbing, carpentering, electrical work, etc.

5. Have an annual examination of the insurance program and shop around for better prices.

6. Check minister's car mileage usage and adjust his or her allowance to the true cost.

7. Seek out ways to save energy through the installation of devices (i.e., clock thermostats).

8. Check out accounts. Are funds being deposited and invested so as to earn interest?

9. Pay bills so as to receive discount for paying within 15-20 days.

10. Seek professional guidance on saving on management and investments.[2]

Every group which handles or controls money should have periodical occasions when the stretching of dollars is the main item of business. Sometimes rather than cut back on mission or ministry, the discovery of new dollar stretching techniques will enable actual increases in ministries. All it takes is the special effort.

The Mission and the Money

Too often those who are responsible for budget management and control are so caught up in the figures and the pressures to keep up buildings that they lose sight of the mission behind it all. As soon as a church becomes nearsighted in this fashion, it begins to lose even the dollars necessary to maintain itself. There is an inextricable linkage between money management and mission enthusiasm. The generous supporters are those who have concern for others.

[2] These suggestions are based on a tape entitled "Money in the Church," made by The Yoke Fellow Institute, Naperville, Illinois, 1978.

Through my years as a pastor, missionary, and administrator, I have discovered that the people who are concerned for mission advancement, both at home and overseas, are those who carry the heaviest load of local church expenses. Even as our Lord said we must lose our lives in order to find them, so local churches discover through mission concerned people that the key to growth is in their own parishes. The heart which is sensitized to the needs of others will contribute enough to cover the basics at the home base.

If your church wants to be around in ten years, then it had better keep track of its money and keep focused on its mission. So, when our Lord said to his twelve disciples, "And preach as you go, saying, 'The kingdom of heaven is at hand.' Heal the sick, raise the dead, cleanse lepers, cast out demons . . ." (Matthew 10:7-8, RSV), he was commissioning them to his highest purpose, the healing of lives and the coming of the kingdom. That trust has been given to us, and the money in our hands is merely one of many tools to enable his plan's completion.

Questions to Ponder or Discuss

1. How does your church membership learn about the budget and expenditures of the church?
2. What kind of budget control form is used in your church? Is it adequate?
3. Do you think a treasurer should meet with your board of trustees? Give reasons for your answer.
4. Can you add some suggestions of how to stretch church dollars without diminishing the church's ministry?

Chapter 5

Buried Treasure for the Kingdom

Tempers were rising at the Doubles' Club annual meeting.

"I'm absolutely opposed to Ralph's suggestion for raising money through our club. As long as I've been a member of First Church, we have resisted all efforts to turn the house of God into a commercial enterprise!" said Judy Somers, as a few other members, sitting near her, nodded with approval.

"Now wait a minute!" protested Ralph Murphy, "I've been around here a while, also. I was only suggesting that our club MIGHT have a bazaar to raise more money for our church! I don't consider that making it a commercial enterprise!

"In fact, any time we raise money for the church, I consider this a spiritual matter! It doesn't make much difference as to how we get the money as long as we don't steal it and it's for God!" At this, some club members applauded.

The president, evidently deciding this issue was dividing the group, banged his gavel and announced, "Ralph's suggestion was given with the best of motives. Judy's right; our church has held down all special, money-raising events like bazaars, fairs, raffles, and dinners for profit. We've always tried to base our financial needs upon voluntary giving.

"But we are a democratic organization, and we must be fair to all our members. So, I'm going to ask a subcommittee to take this issue under advisement and report back to us at our next quarterly business meeting."

At the meal which followed, the main topic of conversation was "Do you agree with Ralph or Judy?"

For Those Responsible for Raising Money

The inevitable question in every organization is: What is the best method for raising the money needed to support the ongoing work and existence of that group? In every organization there are some persons upon whom the burden of responsibility falls for the raising of income. This is also true for the church.

In some churches there is a special stewardship or finance committee responsible for raising the church's money. In other churches, this responsibility falls to the board of trustees. Whichever way it may be in your church, there is still a need for every board to face this crucial question: How do you generate financial support within a local church?

Since the day the early church was founded, the members and leaders of the local congregations have had to struggle with the question of raising money to carry out the ministry and mission of the church.

For the first three hundred years of its history the Christian church raised money through direct gifts and offerings from its members. It also received a portion of crops and other firstfruits of the land. Early wealthy members gave endowments, in the form of property, to perpetuate the work.

From the beginning, the need of money for helping the sick and supporting those early established hospitals, coupled with the need for ways by which to help the poor and the entrapped, was a motivation for giving. The need for support and travel expenses for the apostles and other church leaders was another reason why the early church solicited money from its members.

The history of the Protestant church informs us of the seventeenth-century custom of requiring tithes, by law, for the support of the clergy and the church. This practice was transferred from England and the continent to the new America. When the Reformation came along and separatist groups like the Quakers, Mennonites, and Anabaptists began to question the relationship between church and state in light of their interpretation of the Bible, they also confronted the matter of a state-sponsored tithing system.

In New England, in spite of the protests from dissenters, the church was supported by the taxation of the citizens. Many people went to the stocks or to jail for their convictions on this matter. The sale or rental of pews then entered the picture, as well as lotteries and subscription lists.

With the course of time, and especially because of the Quaker and Baptist confrontation of the state-supported churches, the system of voluntary giving became an established aspect of the American church.

Today, in every church in this country, Roman Catholic or Protestant, the most common form of raising money through the local church is through voluntary giving. In fact this is such an established fact in the American way of life that the United States government allows tax deductions for such giving.

Every board or committee responsible for securing money to support the local church's budget ought to be aware of the history and background of church giving and its implications for them as they seek to implement their responsibilities. That board of trustees, or the stewardship committee, must answer the questions raised by Ralph and Judy. Those persons have been entrusted with a task which affects everyone in that church; the techniques and methods they decide upon impinge upon individual wills and pocketbooks. So, as they are trustees of money control and money spending, they are trustees of money raising. What is God's will for the church? What does God's Word have to say about it? These questions are as important to answer as the questions of deficit or balanced budgets.

The Theology Behind Giving

Every trustee of a local church ought to be well grounded in a biblical understanding of what is basic to the individual Christian concerning his or her use of money.

Jesus taught his disciples that what they did with their money reflected their relationships with God and with other people. As there is an optic nerve between the brain and the eye, so there is a spiritual nerve between the soul and the pocketbook.

The Master taught "Do not lay up for yourselves treasures on earth, where moth and rust consume and where thieves break in and steal. . . . For where your treasure is, there will your heart be also" (Matthew 6:19, 21, RSV).

A board of trustees or the stewardship committee has taken upon itself a responsibility to offer the channels through which those treasures, buried within the lives of Christ's followers, or in the pocketbooks and banks of God's children, find their way into the kingdom work.

When a child of God expresses love to the Father, it is out of the sense of forgiveness which one has experienced. The love of God is forgiving; and the love of God is shared for-giving, which results in giving-for! Our worship, prayer, and walk with God are centered in God's giving of himself, and this results in our giving for God's purposes and plans. The challenging of church members to support a church budget is not in the same category as the club dues, or community taxes. God has shared his treasure with us, and only as we share our treasure in return can there be the true fellowship of love and service.

Giving is voluntary in the church. But, paradoxically, it is not. The story is told of the man who was asked why he didn't give to his church. His response was, "Well, the Lord isn't pressing me like the rest of my creditors!" Where the love of Christ is truly aglow within the human heart, there is a feeling of voluntary compulsion to love and give as he loved and gave to us.

Every member of a church board should be vitally concerned in the total involvement of each member in the church. This goes beyond paying the bills each month, balancing the budget each year, or increasing the size and reach of the church buildings. To set the example of putting one's own treasure in the hands of God is to serve as a witness and enabler for others to experience the joy that is found in Christian giving. It also means that once this life is over, the real treasure in heaven becomes a reality.

In Henry Van Dyke's story, "The Mansion," you will recall a rich man had his mansion on earth but only a tiny hut when he reached heaven. By contrast, a poor Christian doctor who gave all he had to serve God and others discovered, upon arriving in heaven, that he had unknowingly forwarded all the necessary materials to build a mansion for himself.

We are not, if we are truly Spirit-filled, interested in having a mansion waiting for us in heaven. But the deeper teaching helps us to stop and think about sitting "loose" in this world and investing in the more eternal aspects of Christ's kingdom. Think through your theology of giving. Make sure you have one!

Methods of Raising Money

Acknowledging that as trustees we do not raise money only to bolster a sagging budget, or to repair a leaking roof, or to perpetuate a long church history, we realize our purpose is the proclamation of the Good News in Jesus Christ and the addressing of human needs as the incarnate presence of God in the world. So, let us look at some methods of money raising.

The most common method for raising money in the local church is the Every Member Canvass. This system came into being in the twentieth century as a means of systematizing and unifying giving.

The Every Member Canvass has taken on many forms and shapes. It is a program whereby every member of a church is asked to respond to local and missionary needs of the church through personal visitation, resulting in pledging.

The preparations for the Every Member Canvass include budget building (the vision and dream of what could happen if Christians cared); the printing of materials and the utilization of these to teach the members about the mission and ministry of the church; the solicitation of members by visitation (or sometimes it is all done by mail); the securing of specific pledges (which are totaled and announced to the membership until the goal is reached); and the distribution of envelopes which become the means by which contributions are brought to the church worship service (some people opt to send a monthly or quarterly check to the church treasurer).

The strengths of the Every Member Canvass are found in the educational and promotional aspects of the system. The church members are given opportunity to think about their own "treasures" and to become aware of what the church is doing with its money. If one invests his or her treasure in the church then, because the heart will be involved with interest and participation, it makes for greater vitality within the church family.

Not every one, even today, is agreed that a specific pledge through an Every Member Canvass is the best method for giving. Many great churches have accomplished fantastic things without pledges, but usually there is a substitute (perhaps an unwritten pledge of a promise and commitment to giving the tithe). This is just another form of a pledge.

Where the pledging system is used, it has enabled churches to project for the year and to have a commitment from members which brings stability.

Most major national denominations have specialists on their staffs who will help set up an Every Member Canvass. Usually when a church contacts a state of regional denominational office, a member of that staff will visit the local church. Those agencies will have current stewardship materials available for study and purchase.

One church in Houston, Texas, has two Every Member Canvasses a year. The first is to challenge people to give their money and the second is to challenge them to pledge specific talents and periods of time for involvement in mission, through their church, out in the community.

Studies show that the average member of the American main-line churches gives less than 2 percent of income to the work of Christ. And this study is based upon the fact that the largest portions of church budgets are given by a relatively small number of people. This means that every board with financial responsibilities has a tremendous task of stewardship education! Someone has said, "We are never born as stewards, or even born again stewards; stewardship is a learned experience."

Another method for raising money in the local church is through the stressing of proportionate giving. In this method one sets aside a specific portion of money for the mission of Christ. One does this *before* any financial claims are made. The fair and just part of this is that it makes for equity among people, regardless of their material possessions.

The Old Testament method of tithing is another form of

proportionate giving. Jesus underscored this in his teachings. Paul expounded upon it. He urged people to lay aside money upon the first day of the week according to the way God had blessed them financially. Some denominations and local churches urge people who are frightened or threatened by tithing (10 percent of an income) to try beginning at a lesser percentage, such as 5 percent or 6 percent. This would at least get people above the low average of 2 percent or less and move them toward greater commitment.

Whatever the method used, the church leadership should make certain that each year special attention be given to rethinking the whole matter of "treasures" and church treasuries. The giver comes nearest to giving self in giving money to the church, and our concern is with people in relationship with God and each other. That puts budget raising on a high, biblical and theological plane.

Other Methods of Raising Money

One of the neglected areas of stewardship is that of deferred giving. Any up-to-date survey of a local church will show that rarely does it enter the minds of those leaders responsible for teaching ways of contributing to God's work to have a plan by which concerned members might think seriously about including their church in their wills. Too often, only the exceedingly rich or affluent are challenged to provide a way to continue contributing after death. But even the most ordinary of us ought to look upon a will as a continuous way of perpetuating a mission concern through the years.

Most churches do not realize the great financial potential

in educating members regarding deferred giving through the inclusion of the church in an individual will. We should be using our newsletters and personal contacts constantly to remind people that they can carry on the ministry and mission of Christ long after leaving this earth.

It is important to instruct people to consult with the local church leadership and especially to avoid the danger of inflexibility in including a church or mission project in a will. A woman died leaving $25,000 to a church to be used for the installation of a women's toilet near the church sanctuary! Obviously the donor resented having to walk to the church basement. But the structure of the church did not provide any place where this wish could be carried out, to say nothing of the fact that the cost would be closer to $3,000 or $4,000. It would have been better to have left this amount as a gift to be used on the church building as the trustees saw specific needs.

Many boards of trustees will be responsible for managing investments that have resulted from bequests left to the church. Often these bequests can increase the annual support of the church program by a considerable annual amount. The danger is that members will cease to give their own proportionate share and will leave more responsibility upon the investments. The way to guard against this is to earmark portions of the invested funds for those projects which would not otherwise be carried out by the church. Of course some bequests will have restrictions upon them and will require the strict adherence to those restrictions by the trustees.

Still other methods of raising money are through gift annuity programs, grants, life insurance, and property. Each denomination has specific information on these methods. Usually, there is at least one skilled individual in each church who can serve to consult and advise. What is important is to remember that sooner or later the trustees or finance committee do become involved in these other methods of fund raising as stewards of the church.

Teaching Mission the Key to Giving

There are still those in the Christian church who believe the key to giving is to teach churches to give as much to others as they use for their own maintenance and programs. Some of the most vital congregations in the country practice this, but they are very few.

Whether giving to others ever achieves the ideal of equal sharing or not, it is a clue to dynamic stewardship. The church which has a deep concern for mission in its own community and in the world will never have to worry about whether or not it will be able to balance its budget or pay its bills.

In most churches the board of Christian education or the missions committee has the responsibility for teaching about mission and generating mission concern. Most boards of trustees consider this to be far away and totally unrelated to them; but it is not! Mission concern is the heartbeat that keeps that blood flowing. And for the board of trustees the money is the lifeblood of the church. Hence, they are inseparable—the beating heart of mission and the life-giving money of people. This means that even trustees need education and motivation in mission. They need to see and feel what dollars do when they move beyond the local church building and transform the hearts and ways of other people. They, too, need to know that buildings and programs of great significance have needs in the inner city, or on the foreign field.

There is a myth abroad that overseas mission is no longer a viable program of the church. This is not true! There may be radical changes taking place as national leadership assumes its rightful control of ministry and mission in other countries. But the dollars are needed there, as much as ever, even as they are needed at the home base. The teaching of Jesus concerning the finding of one's life by losing it applies as much to churches as it does to people. As the heart of God is involved in Africa, Asia, or Latin America, in selfless love, so too must our treasures be shared with the larger family of the Father, if we want to stay in business. Any quick study of healthy churches which do not have financial problems of their own will quickly show that those churches are concerned for people *everywhere*. They have personalized mission and taken upon themselves the task of assuming the burden of God's world—through the sharing distribution of their treasure!

It occurred to me as I visited with a number of boards of trustees that it would be a good idea to have a few moments of devotional thought at the opening of the session related to mission. Why not read a letter from an Indian-American in mission? Or take three minutes to tell about that special need in Zaire? Boards of trustees could be enabled to have a wider perspective on mission which in turn will help them as they sense anew their part in digging up the treasure of God's eternal love and distributing it to the wider world.

Questions to Ponder or Discuss

1. If you were on the Doubles' Club board, how would you have responded to Ralph's suggestion?
2. How do you respond to the idea of proportionate giving?
3. What is your church doing about helping others to include God's work in their wills?
4. Think or talk about the statement "They are inseparable, the beating heart of mission and the life-giving money of people."

Chapter 6

Working with the Professional Team

The pastoral relations committee looked grim as it sat with its pastor. At least this was the feeling that the minister got as she met with them for the first annual evaluation session.

"Rev. Baxter, the other three members and I have been looking forward to this get-together," the moderator began.

Liz Baxter couldn't be sure whether she was reading something ominous into the opening statement or not. She surveyed the faces of the others as Moderator Kurt Paulson opened the meeting.

Perhaps, she tried to tell herself, the anxieties she had about this first such meeting were due to a touch of amateur paranoia. She imagined this must be the way every young minister feels in his or her first pastorate.

As he opened a manila folder with businesslike precision, Moderator Paulson continued: "We thought the best way to begin this evaluation session is to ask you to tell us how you feel about Calvary Presbyterian at the end of your first year. Are things going well from your perspective? Are you happy; are we measuring up to your expectations?"

The Reverend Elizabeth Baxter felt a wave of peace and reassurance at this positive approach. Kurt's tone of voice allayed her fears. She wanted to share the good things that she felt. Oh, there were some things she could have done without, but it had been a good year. She felt confident now that this evaluation would end on a positive note.

When she finished sharing her views on the year and assuring the committee that harmony existed and the work at Calvary Presbyterian was moving forward, Bill Goodyear spoke up adding his commendations concerning her ministry: "We like your preaching. It's well prepared, provocative, and uplifting. The church school looks healthy. And the young people are responding to your sensitivity and openness to them. . . ."

Liz looked at the others as he spoke, and they all nodded with agreement.

"But, we do have a concern. . . ."

Here it comes; things were all too perfect. In fact she remembered the words, at that moment, of dear old Professor Donahue, who reminded the seminary seniors in their Pastoral Care class that any year which had nothing but positive critiques might be an indication of future, serious trouble.

"Our concern," chimed in Doris Springer, "is in the area of administration. We wonder if you enjoy that part of church work."

"Well," began the minister, with some struggling for words, "let's say it isn't the area of church work in which I feel most comfortable. But, neither is working mechanically on my car, even though I love to drive it."

"We understand," answered Doris with the feeling that her minister might now be showing some defensiveness. "We don't expect you to ring the bell in all aspects of the church life, but there have been some things arise that we want to talk about with you." With this, she looked toward Tony Ferrelli, chairman of the board of trustees.

Picking up the signal, Tony looked into his pastor's eyes and said, "Reverend Baxter, the trustees are concerned that you rarely come to our meetings."

Is that all it is? thought Liz. *Then that one I can answer easily.*

"My feeling is that we have an excellent board of trustees," she said. "It's true, I have not been to all their meetings because I honestly felt that they didn't need me. Tony has prepared good agendas, and he and I have talked together about them. And then, after the meetings, we have touched base with each other about the highlights and decisions made."

Looking at Tony, she said, "You never told me it bothered you—that is—my not being at your meetings."

"It doesn't bother me," Tony responded, "but some of the trustees told me, as I prepared for this evaluating session, that it bothers them. They say you should be there at all times. They say it is the minister's job."

"Well, I don't agree," Bill Goodson broke in. "Ministers are neither trained nor qualified to meet with the trustees. Why should they waste their time? Our pastor is concentrating on ministry and Christian education; those are the spiritual matters for which she was called and prepared. That ought to be enough. Let the trustees do their work without imposing upon the minister. I just think that's good stewardship of time and energy."

Liz liked Bill's defense. The others didn't seem too sure.

The Minister as Executive Manager

The minister of the local church is the executive manager of that body. The trustees are those who manage for others, or who hold title on behalf of others; so the minister is the person responsible for administering them. We might note that the word "administer" really means to serve as the minister with the added responsibility of conducting and controlling the affairs of the body.

Some ministers do not want to be administrators or executive managers; they insist their call was to the prophetic and priestly functions. However, these persons soon learn that the church is an organization with various working parts. Even though there are groups like deacons, elders, boards of Christian education or missions, or boards of trustees or finance, someone has to assume the role of catalytic agent to bring them together as one functioning body. The minister is that person who brings holism to the church as well as holiness. The minister is responsible to the church as a president of a company is responsible to the stockholders. Thus, the minister must work with each individual part of the church as a company general manager or president must work with all aspects of his or her company's organization.

Jesus was not only the Teacher and Master for the disciples, but he was also their executive manager. He served to keep them together and inspired (Matthew 4:18-25). He made certain they had proper instructions in terms of attitudes and behavior (Matthew 5 and 6). He instructed them how to go out and sell the "Good News" (Matthew 10:1-42). We know that even the simple organization of apostles with twelve members had a treasurer in the person of Judas. And after our Lord was taken up to heaven, the apostles reorganized with a replacement for Judas (Acts 1:12-26) and it is apparent that Peter took over as the executive manager.

To belittle executive responsibilities in ministry is to have a fractional view of the total work of the church. The executive-manager minister is the team captain who serves as the instrumentality through which kingdom action takes place corporately. It requires spiritual commitment, the willingness to work with the details of administration, and openness in guiding people toward the fulfillment of the goals set by the local church.

In visiting with boards of trustees, it was amazing to me to discover how many ministers do not bother to attend the meetings of those boards because they do not feel it is part of their responsibility. So, let me share why I believe every minister should be at the board of trustees' meetings:

1. *Because the minister is the resident theologian of the church.* This means the minister, above all other members of that church, ought to be present and available at all times to give a biblical and theological rationale for those issues which may arise, i.e., use of the church by outside groups, division of money to social or mission causes; the reasons behind mission or Christian education issues which require judgments or actions by the trustees.

2. *Because the minister is the switchboard communicator.* Usually the only person in the church who has the overview of all the boards and committees of the corporation is the minister. If the board of Christian education needs new chairs or the women's group wants to meet an emergency need in the hunger area, the minister can be supportive of those groups even though a special person may be sent to meet with the board of trustees.

Another very important reason for the minister's presence is that he or she will be the one meeting with the nominating committee to consider the need of continuing or replacing members of that board. The minister will have invaluable information for the nominating committee. But it will only be available if the minister has maintained an ongoing, personal relationship with members of the board.

Sometimes it will be impossible for a minister to attend a board of trustees meeting. In these cases the minister should have a thorough discussion with the chairperson, before and after the meeting. Some ministers have solved this problem of absence by having a cassette or tape recording of the session.

3. *Because the minister is the preacher-interpreter for the whole church.* Being the only person who speaks to the congregation each week provides the minister with a unique opportunity to interpret the actions of the boards to the people. This means the functions of these boards are always held up as Christian service and included as forms of ministry and mission. The encouragement of reminding people that the hard work of trustees, who handle books and paint buildings, is another vital aspect of Christian action

which will serve to help those trustees realize that they are important members of Christ's body.

4. *Because the minister is the public relations person of the church.* Whether it is through the Sunday bulletin or a weekly or monthly news mailing, the minister is the one who is able to pass on information from each board to the church constituency. Many items which boards of trustees touch upon are totally unknown by the church members.

I remember visiting with one board of trustees in a church I happen to know very well. The bulk of the meeting was related to a number of serious problems in the church building. The key to it all was finding the money to make some major changes in the building. I had the feeling that if the church members had known how serious the building problems were, they would have responded with extra gifts of money. But the minister wasn't there, and no one volunteered to get the word out to others. That responsibility resides with the executive manager. This doesn't mean the minister does all the work, or even all the publicizing. It does mean, however, that the minister will make certain someone does it.

The Minister and the Board of Trustees as a Team

A minister's ability to be a leader is tested out at the point of effectiveness in working with church boards and committees. Even though the minister is the executive-manager of the church, he or she must know how to work democratically with those boards. A good executive never rides roughshod over his or her comanagers and workers. Each member of the board of trustees was selected to serve because the church body decided there was something to be gained from each. So, the minister needs to know how to work with such people and how to bring out to a maximum the gifts which each person possesses. The wise minister will be constantly on the lookout for members to be recommended to be on the board of trustees. After a few years that minister should have a team which will work with the minister, but not necessarily rubber-stamp every ministerial whim or desire.

It is extremely important that the minister and the chairperson of the board of trustees keep in constant contact. Perhaps an occasional lunch together, or an invitation to dinner at home will help to create an understanding between human beings and followers in Christ.

The Board of Trustees and the Church Staff

Even though the minister is the executive-manager, every board in the church is made up of the stockholders of the corporation to which the minister is responsible. So the relationship is two-way. The board of trustees not only is responsible for the church building and its maintenance, but also it has a unique relationship to the employees of that church.

In many churches the board of trustees sets the salaries of the staff. That's enough to create potential conflict. But, the trustees make more decisions than that, which could lead to conflict. They are responsible for the care and upkeep of the parsonage or manse. They often determine whether there is money enough for a full-time secretary, or an associate, or the new copy machine. This means the board of trustees probably makes more decisions affecting staff fulfillment, and staff efficiency and peace of mind, than any other church board.

If a church is small and has only a minister, custodian, and organist, the board of trustees will act upon salaries, equipment available, and the times which the church building will be used. If it is a larger church with a multiple staff, some of these decisions may be made by a church cabinet or council, or a special personnel committee. Even so, undoubtedly there will be one member of the board of trustees on that decision-making committee.

Many churches have a pastoral (or ministerial) relations committee which meets regularly with the minister or other members of the ministerial staff for evaluation. Often a member of the board of trustees (perhaps the chairperson) is on the pastoral relations committee because questions of salary scales, increment, and housing concerns will arise.

As churches grow larger, many times they add business managers to their staffs. Where this has happened, it often means the senior minister has less direct relationship with the board of trustees because the business manager fills this gap. I would still hope that the minister would attend the board of trustees' meeting at least three or four times a year and, in the meantime, keep in very close touch with what is going on through the business manager.

Because the custodial work of the church is under the board of trustees, the custodian or superintendent of buildings is directly responsible to that board. My experience has shown that too few boards of trustees ever invite a custodian or superintendent of buildings to sit in on an occasional meeting to find out how this person is thinking, feeling, or sometimes hurting. All of us have learned that custodial people take a great deal of abuse from insensitive church members. Our task, when there is a multiple staff, is to be sensitive to the team relationship and how we can help it attain greater unity and cooperation.

Finally, one thing a board of trustees must always keep in mind is that the minister is the chief staff person. If a board finds a conflict between any two staff persons of the church, it should always be certain that the senior minister is aware and is a part of all efforts to bring about unity. The minister should be consulted on any and all staff problems which may be brought to a board of trustees. Anything less than this can result in divisiveness in the staff and even in the church.

Questions to Ponder or Discuss

1. What do you think of the idea that the minister is an executive-manager? Do you agree or not?
2. Should the board of trustees be involved in a pastoral relations committee? Give reasons for your answer.
3. What if there was trouble with the custodian or superintendent of buildings in your church; who would handle the situation?

Chapter 7

Trustees in a Changing World

April and Charlie Newman were enjoying their candle-light dinner with Joe and Sally Cobb. It was always a pleasure to get together. They had been doing this, almost weekly, since they met at the Couples' Club at church.

"Hey, Charlie," exclaimed Joe, between bites, "how are the meetings going at the board of trustees?"

"Well," replied Charlie, "it's been a shocking experience for me. You know, I served on the trustee board for two terms, and was even chairman; but that was a long time ago. In fact, I haven't been on the board or even in touch with them for almost fourteen years."

"Things haven't changed that much," chimed in Sally as she poured the coffee. "Trustees are trustees, whether then or now!"

"Yeh, the job description's the same: care for the building and grounds; control the money; keep an eye on the investments—all that stuff. But, we're living in a different world. We're running into things that we never thought of fourteen years ago. The world has changed," responded Charlie.

To which April exclaimed, "You can say that again!"

The Newmans and the Cobbs were facing a reality which engulfs everyone today. We are living in a time of rapid, radical change.

The rapidly shrinking world, brought about by communication and travel, has resulted in instant economic effects which cause quick changes in money values and money management.

The overcrowded world has brought about the need for greater sensitivity to people who are different, or who are caught in the traps set by the thoughtless majorities. This is resulting in new laws which impinge upon the old ways.

The worn-out world has brought about a new need for evaluating the utilization of the world's resources. No longer can people or groups ignore the rapidly dwindling supplies of energy, which everyone has taken for granted. The fast-growing computer world is bringing about changes in methods of management and ways of living which boggle the mind.

Charlie Newman was right. The board of trustees of today is not the same as that of fourteen years ago. New problems have arisen; new social implications exist; new crises face the church; and new methods for resolution are necessary.

Trustees of churches are discovering that they cannot separate the trust which has been laid upon them by the membership from the trust which they likewise hold regarding the world's direction and future. The day when trustees could put on blinders and give attention only to the building, budget, and bank has gone! As Christians who have assumed the maintenance and management responsibilities of the church, they also have a prior responsibility always to remember they are accountable for the maintenance and management of the world God so loves!

Let us look at those areas which trustees encounter:

You Can't Escape the Energy Problems

For the last several decades the United States increasingly has built its way of life around oil and natural gas. It has fueled its homes, schools, churches, automobiles, and industries with cheap oil from overseas and from our own continental resources. But, unfortunately, we have forgotten that oil and natural gas are nonrenewable resources. The world's supply, and even that of the United States, will eventually diminish and be lost. Even as frantic efforts are made to discover new sources under the seas, or under the ice, the expenses are rising at a rate where it will eventually be unprofitable to continue seeking new places from which to extract the oil.

In the light of this energy change it is important to ask, "What are the churches doing to conserve energy?" A survey was done by the national executives of nine denominations who joined as an Energy Research Work Group, under the auspices of the Joint Strategy and Action Committee, Inc., a New York-based ecumenical agency. In making their report, the *JSAC Grapevine* writes:

> During the last five years the cost of fuel oil has more than doubled and other energy costs have soared.
> • How have the programs and budgets of local congregations been affected by this unprecedented increase in the cost of fuel and energy?

- How has the higher cost of energy affected benevolence giving?
- To what extent have members of congregations wrestled with the implications of dwindling, non-renewable fossil fuels for their theology and life styles as Christians?
- Are congregations with large memberships affected more or less than small congregations?
- Is the response different in any given location for Southern Baptists as compared to American Lutherans or United Methodists?

These and other questions were asked by the national church development executives from more than a dozen denominations as they worked together in the JSAC Church Development Task Force.[1]

The congregations were asked, "What changes, since 1972, have been made in the physical plant of your church to conserve energy?" The answer from most was, "Adjust the thermostat!" Fifty-five out of 241 congregations said they had done nothing at all. The report reminds us that adjusting the thermostat is the most cost-effective measure there is. A change of only five degrees in thermostat settings either for heating or for cooling a church can result in considerable savings.

This survey also revealed that only half of the churches had made any major expenditures to change their physical plant for energy-related purposes. It appeared there was at least a two-year lag in the response made to the energy problem by congregations.

Every board of trustees, or church property committee, has a responsibility to focus attention of the entire

[1] *JSAC Grapevine,* Joint Strategy and Action Committee, Inc., vol. 9, no. 5 (December, 1977), p. 1.

membership on the question of use of energy in the church building or buildings.

See recommendations in Appendix B to help your board in energy conservation.

A board of trustees which takes seriously its place in the life of the church and the community will make every effort to investigate every potential for energy conservation. This will result in curbing costs and in releasing fuels for other greater needs.

Inflation Is Here to Stay

A group of ministers were meeting with a pension-fund executive to talk about planning for the future. The executive took the base salary of one of the younger ministers, which at the time was at $8,000, and calculated his salary for the year 2010 when he would retire. Figuring a modest inflationary increase of 5 percent per year, it came to an annual wage of over $50,000! This was a simple, but shocking, example of what inflation is doing. If that salary figure was 20 percent of the church's total budget, then the budget would be $250,000!

It is precisely because of this inflation that boards of trustees and/or financial officers must get churches to do long-range planning and to determine what those projections signify to the members relative to budget controls and budget raising.

There must be a prayerful evelution of church programs, their effect, their reason for being, and their projected time of life.

There should be analyses of staff functions and the need

for such staff. Some churches with multiple staffs can no longer afford the luxury of delegated ministry. Some professional functions may have to be taken over by volunteers.

There should be a diagnosis of the meetings of groups at the church. Perhaps small groups could now meet in private homes. This would be another way to overcome the fuel-energy crisis as well.

Certainly the trustees and other officers of the church should work hard at communicating with the membership regarding the impact of inflation on the ministry and mission of the church. We are living in an affluent society, and the church members will help to meet the inflationary costs if they are properly informed and challenged.

The real key to overcoming the potential handicapping of the inflationary disease is to stress commitment to Jesus Christ and his church. That's all the more reason why trustees must not only stress commitment in others but manifest it in their own lives as well.

Regulations Are Meant to Help Us

Another new dimension in the life of the church is its being required to pay more attention to regulations set down by the community. These will come, especially, from health departments, fire departments, and building inspectors.

Many church people consider regulatory mandates as a nuisance, but the fact is most of them are meant to help us all. Since, as churches, we open our doors to the public, we therefore have a responsibility to conform to those regulations which are created for the public's well-being.

Every board of trustees, or property committee, should have at least one member who is familiar with the changing regulations which emerge in every community. If such a person is not available then, perhaps someone will volunteer to become the "regulatory liaison" and make an effort to become informed—especially in the areas of health, safety, and building codes. Some communities may have a group or organization which will help any church interested to discover what the latest regulations are and how to check out a building's acceptability as related to those codes. (See Appendix C for a sample checklist.)

Make Way for the Aged and Handicapped

There is a new raising of consciousness concerning the special needs of people who are older in terms of years and those who have physical handicaps.

Too rarely do churches ask themselves whether someone in a wheelchair, or using a cane, can negotiate the stairs, or even sing in the choir. How many minutes are spent in a board of trustees' meeting on the question of proper lighting in the sanctuary so people with poor eyesight can read the litany or hymns? And what about the hard of hearing? Have we wired certain pews for individual P.A. headsets?

Some communities are establishing regulations to require churches to have ramps for the handicapped or special parking areas with signs designating their availability for those who cannot walk distances or who may be confined to wheelchairs.

Barrier-free architecture has now come into its own. We have come to realize that there has been insensitivity in churches to the "over 65" segment of society, or to the physically handicapped. We didn't realize that so many barriers were constructed and allowed to continue until the vocal senior adults and wheelchair occupants became militant. They called our attention to the many physical inconveniences which we tended to overlook.

Every church should take time to survey its properties in the light of the needs of the physically handicapped. The following are some of the questions which should be asked:

* Are parking areas large enough? All individual spaces should be at least nine feet wide so people can get in and out of cars easily.

* Is there a four-foot width walk at each end of the parking lot for the loading and unloading of wheelchairs?

* Are all the walks paved? If so, are they smooth so that a person will not stumble or fall?

* Are there any signs, parking meters, or other obstructions which may prove to be a problem for the blind?

* Do your steps have contrasting colors? Have you provided nonslip surfaces? Are there handrails?

* Are all your doors three feet wide? Do they have vision panels and panic (push-bar) hardware?

* Are all corridors clear of obstacles, such as coatracks, drinking fountains, and loose clutter that could trip the blind?

* Is there a ramp for wheelchair persons with ample room on the latching side of the door to allow opening of the door?

These are just a sample of the many questions that boards of trustees and property committees ought to be asking themselves.

The elderly who have difficulty walking and the handicapped of sight, hearing, or body are also members of the Body of Christ. They too have a need to gather with the gathered church. If there is no place in the sanctuary for the placing of a wheelchair, or the enabling of the hard of hearing, they will get the message very clearly. But, since we are a caring extension of the caring Master, we will do everything within our power to include people with special needs. This will require special attention and expenditures by the board of trustees.

The Age of Grievance Groups

What would happen in your church if a group of people, who were not members, descended upon it and demanded the right to speak from the pulpit on an issue or to confront the church members within their building? Could you respond responsibly and redemptively or would your trustees call the police?

When James Forman presented his demands at Riverside Church, he presented some issues to that board of trustees that previous boards had never faced. He confronted the questions of racism and poverty and linked them to financial resources in the local church. He raised the question of whether any local church property, fund, or people were free from the impingements of social justice.

The day of demands is as old as the Old Testament, or Martin Luther; it will not disappear because a local church insists that it has complete freedom from the cry of the powerless. To think that the voiceless will not raise their voices again is as ridiculous as to think that earthquakes will not move the earth because we have been through them before. Demands will come again; the powerless and voiceless will continue to seek ways to overcome hurts, wrongs, and injustices.

What should a board of trustees do if the church is confronted by a group with demands? The following suggestions are given:

1. Have a meeting of the official body of the church. Hear the whole story; do not make judgments until there has been time to listen to the complaining group.

2. Set a specific time and place to hear the other viewpoint.

3. Make an effort to identify the scope of the concern. How many people does this concern?

4. Try to look beyond the words that are being spoken. What lies behind these demands; what do they symbolize?

5. Provide a procedure for responding. What is reasonable? What is just? What is Christian?

6. Finally, what do these protests say about our buildings, possessions, and resources? Perhaps they mean we should provide a regular meeting place, with a caring atmosphere.

Dealing with these issues is not only the responsibility of the deacons or elders. The board of trustees, as stewards of all the external aspects of the church, likewise must come to grips with the theological and social implications which have arisen.

The Church and Disaster Response

Every so often a church is confronted with a nearby disaster. Perhaps it is a flood, tornado, earthquake, or fire.

Sometimes, in the north, an ice storm or heavy snow tears down electric wires so that whole communities are without light and heat. This means that the Red Cross, or some other Civil Response unit, is looking for buildings to use where beds can be set up, warmth and food can be provided, and lives can be saved.

Every church should take a vote in advance that instructs its trustees to respond to such needs. Sometimes a public official contacts a church official asking for use of the building during the emergency only to be told there is a need for a church vote. Let the church make a vote in advance.

Then the board of trustees should survey its property and ask itself how it can be ready for such an emergency. It may store some blankets, cots, extra clothing, flashlights, and canned foods, just in case. At the very least it should draw up a mimeographed plan of the building which indicates its potential.

In this way it could tell the Red Cross, upon inquiry, that it could accommodate one hundred people in the social hall; that a kitchen is there with all the dishes and paraphernalia needed to feed the group; and that toilets are adequate.

Every community faces the possibility of a natural emergency or one brought on by human carelessness. Every church, through its board of trustees, should ask itself how it would respond. In mission concern the church should be ready.

The Church and Public Social Responsibility

Gone is the day when a board of trustees only has to think of its responsibility to those who respond to the church bell and sit in the pews on a Sunday morning! The good old days of preaching individual morality and repentance have now moved to the challenge of confronting corporate sin and the need for corporate repentance. The business community is now being confronted with the issue of public social responsibility, and this puts the church trustees also in the penetrating light of the gospel.

At a meeting of the 28th General Synod of the Anglican Church of Canada, a Christian businessman by the name of E. G. Pullen is reported as having

> given the Church a sound theological reason why it had no choice but to speak out loudly against injustice. A member of the controversial Public Social Responsibility (PSR) Unit which oversees for the Anglican Church its involvement with such interchurch projects as GATT-Fly, the Task Force on Churches and Corporate Responsibility and Project North, Mr. Pullen said that for too long the church has been, "truly the opiate of the masses and not its needle." [2]

Why the sudden interest in corporate responsibility and what does it have to do with a board of trustees? The answer is that the small, shrinking, dying world we live in has forced us as churches to look at questions concerning environment and world development. Churches are corporations which hold investments, and the managers of those investments have a Christian social obligation to utilize the power in that money for the uplift of peoples and nations.

Many denominations and churches are taking seriously their corporate social responsibility and are looking at companies, of which they are part owners, to determine

[2] *The Ecumenist,* vol. 16, no. 1 (November and December, 1977), p. 2.

whether racism, injustice, housing, welfare, minority rights, and health are deemed as social areas where the company is sensitive and responsive. The gospel of justice and liberation is the concern of many churches, and because they are taking this seriously, they want those who have been entrusted with their money also to take it seriously. In the new age in which we live there is a greater desire on the part of many Christians to insist upon a stronger critique of every aspect of life, both individual and corporate, in the light of the Bible and of Christian faith.

Boards of trustees are not only responsible for the land around their churches, but they are also bearers of responsibility for the land being ruined in the next state or country by those who are motivated only by profit and not the welfare of generations to come. They not only are charged with the need of budget control and wise spending but also with the need for concern for those who control the world's wealth at the expense of the world's poor. It is a different day in which we live, and public social responsibility is a part of the difference.

Questions to Ponder or Discuss

1. What are five ways a church can save energy?
2. Can you name some of the regulations for public buildings (churches) in effect in your community?
3. Can you see at least three obstacles to the handicapped in your church? What could be done to remedy them?

Chapter 8

You Learn Through Others

Many well-qualified people who have the potential for making good trustees have been lost to the church because they were frightened off by the magnitude of the job offered. It may have been more a fear of the unknown than anything—especially if one has not been properly informed about trustees' work. There really is only one way to learn how to be a trustee and that is to be one. We learn by doing! But, the risk is so high that most of us will shy away from the challenge.

The second best thing then is to learn through the experience of others. One of the most effective ways is to peek through a keyhole while an actual board is meeting. This enables one to have some ideas as to the functions, styles, and methods used by others.

So, on your behalf, I met with various church trustee boards as a silent observer. I also interviewed members and chairpersons of some boards. All of this data is put together in this chapter to help you get an inside look at how trustees carry out their meetings today.

The names in the following case studies are fictional, but

the case studies themselves are based on actual materials gathered from the people interviewed and the meetings attended.

Case Study No. I—The Trinity Methodist Church

The meeting opens with a brief prayer which is offered by the minister. There are six men, plus the pastor, and two women present.

The minutes of the last meeting are read by the secretary; and there is some discussion of items in those minutes, i.e., neighbors using the church parking lot during snowstorms. Now that spring has come, this is no longer a problem.

The chairman, Sam, says the "old business" would include committee reports. The House Committee reports on the progress of cleaning certain carpets.

Another board member brings up the matter of water seeping into the basement of the church. Discussion centers around the cause. It was caused, says one, by the ramp installed into the basement; another suggests it was caused by water from the roof going into the dry-wells and causing an overflow. One person suggests that the gutters should be changed, especially the "leader."

"What's a 'leader'?" asks one of the members.

"That's a downspout," explains another.

Finally, Bill offers to find someone to do this work. He will get estimates for the next meeting.

The next item of old business is the repair of the fence. Susan reports that it has been done.

Under "new business" the chairman reads a report from the treasurer informing them that the utility bill from

January 1 to April 1 is $4,263.40! He observes that expenses are running 5 percent over a year ago! All agree that it is normal inflation.

A toilet needs repairing in the educational building and Joe offers to fix it.

The members respond to Chairman Sam's next item of business concerning the Spring Workday. They discuss the need for assigning volunteers for specific tasks to be done. The minister says some people come each year to do the same job, such as raking, window washings, etc.

A date is set for May with suggestions on what needs to be done, who will buy the supplies.

Susan volunteers to get a few folk to help her make phone calls to potential volunteers and says she will get some women to prepare coffee and lunch.

The next item on the agenda concerns a contact from City Hall relative to the installation of a chairlift for the elderly and handicapped. City Hall officials say the inspector reported that the church failed to get a permit for this. Sam said the contractor was responsible for seeing about the permit. Chuck offers to check with the contractor.

Chairman Sam says he was phoned by a gentleman who wants to rent the social hall for the purpose of giving trumpet lessons and eventually starting a brass band. Those present feel there is no time for another group in the church. A band would disturb other meetings taking place simultaneously.

Since there is no other business, the meeting is adjourned.

Evaluation

This was a well-run meeting, which began on time, with an

agenda in mind. It would have been better, however, to have had an agenda for each person present.

Everyone present took part. When one member did not understand about "leaders" and spout run-offs, the chairman gave time to allow an explanation.

It appeared that each of those present, men and women alike, were picking up delegated responsibilities and reporting on them back to the board.

One impression I received was that this whole meeting was strictly "building oriented." At no time was there a holistic relationship to worship, education, fellowship, or the mission of the church. For example, perhaps there could have been more investigation of the matter of renting the social hall for the gentleman who wanted to start a band. No one suggested that there should be input from the Christian education committee or the outreach committee. Maybe this was an opening for a greater mission relationship to the community.

Case Study No. II—First Baptist Church of Red River

This meeting was held at 9:00 P.M. immediately after a Lenten Service. The chairman, Mr. Chester Sennett, is an elderly, retired businessman. He opens the meeting with apologies for calling it after this Lenten Service, but he explains that everyone is so busy that he thought it best to do it this way. One woman, four other men, and the pastor are present.

The chairman, Mr. Sennett, says the secretary is absent so they will dispense with minutes. Can anyone remember what they touched on last time?

Mrs. Johnson says she remembers the discussion about the need for better coat-hanging facilities in the front hall. The children who come in cannot reach the hooks. One of the men present offers to do something about this, since nothing has yet happened.

Another trustee remembers that there was concern about the church kitchen. As it is being used more and more, there is less and less volunteering to give it some special cleaning. Mr. Sennett asks, "Who is looking after that?" No one seems to know; but one person thinks it is June Chaffee who couldn't be present tonight. He will get in touch with her.

With summer coming, the chairman points out that the old lawnmower they've been nursing along for many summers has now died! Who will look into prices? There is money in the budget, Russ Smith reminds them. No one responds. Finally, the pastor says, "There's a nice shop on the outskirts of town. I'll look in there and see if I can get a good price." All agree this is a good idea.

"Is there any other new business?" asks Chairman Sennett.

"Some of us would like to see a soda pop machine in the social hall," volunteers Russ Smith.

A discussion takes place concerning the advantages and disadvantages of such a dispensing machine. One points out that with the Weight-Watchers' club using that hall, it should handle only diet sodas. This is noted in the minutes; and they move on to other items.

Mr. Thompson speaks up and asks what has happened to the plans to move the church building back from the highway? No one seems to know. Mrs. Johnson says she remembers that this was an item which the Long-Range

Planning Committee was considering. Does anyone know what conclusions they have come to? No one responds.

The Reverend Mr. Phelps says, "According to the bylaws of our church, the Long-Range Planning Committee should be taking some action on this."

To this Russ Smith responds, "I thought the Long-Range Planning Committee's role was purely spiritual and our job is strictly the building."

"No," responds the pastor, "their job is to plan for all aspects of the church's life."

Mrs. Johnson breaks in, "The parsonage needs painting very badly. It is peeling in many places."

Discussion of how often you paint a parsonage, and whether you do one side a year, takes place.

It is agreed that the leaking church roof is far more of a problem for now, so attention should be given to that. Since the Ladies' Class has donated $3,000 for the roof repair, this should be done first. Mr. Thompson suggests that a "paint-the-parsonage" fund could be established.

After a number of other small matters are discussed, the chairman calls for closing the meeting.

The Reverend Mr. Phelps speaks up and says, "I have one other matter. We need to buy new church school curriculum, but we don't know how much money we are allowed." The chairman responds, "I'll call you from home and let you know." And the meeting ends.

Evaluation

The choice of time of the meeting was poor. To change from a regular night for the convenience of a few is not good.

Also, to have a back-to-back meeting is to put a time pressure on people.

With the secretary being absent, someone should have made an effort to get at least one copy of the minutes from the last meeting.

The chairman did not have an agenda prepared, and thus they wandered from item to item without consideration of priority matters. Perhaps the moving of the church should have been given much more time.

The member trustees were aware of needs of the church properties, but they did not volunteer to pursue individual concerns as they should have. When no one took up the "lawnmower" purchase, the pastor jumped in. He should not have felt this pressure of obligation.

The matter of the Long-Range Planning Committee's responsibility for making plans for the future actions of the church raised the old question of what is spiritual and what is secular within the life of the church. It revealed a need within the membership to face issues of the holistic, spiritual life of all the boards.

Finally, the pastor's need to raise the question of money for church school curriculum showed this board approves all expenditures (though nothing was said about this in the meeting). But there was no copy of the budget there, nor any sign of close communication with the church treasurer.

Case Study No. III—St. Thomas Episcopal Church

The meeting is opened by Mr. Clarence Brown, a school teacher in his thirties. The other six members are Miss Sally Nolan, a retired telephone operator; Stan Emerson, who is not present tonight; Jim O'Leary, an energetic young contractor; Joan Seeley, who says she's "just a housewife"; Charlie Daly, a middle-aged carpenter; and Bill Peters, a telephone company executive. The minister, Father Goodrich, comes in late.

Mr. Brown opens the meeting with prayer and then announces what the agenda will be:

The Secretary's Report

The Treasurer's Report

Old Business

Report of Progress on Painting the Walls in the Halls of the Church Manse (Parsonage)

Report on Complaints About the Custodial Care

Report on the Budget Now Being Prepared for Next Year

Other Business that Trustees Feel Should Be Acted Upon

After the reports are read by Miss Nolan, the group plunges into discussion of the painting of the manse. Mr. Brown explains that he and two other folk have completed that project.

The chairman reminds the group that there has been considerable criticism of the custodial work.

Someone asks if there is a job description, to which Bill Peters says, "Yes, I have one at my house."

Joan Seeley says she understands the custodian does not wash and wax the floors regularly. "He should," says Bill Peters, "it's in his job description."

"And didn't we just give him a raise recently?" asks Joan. All present nod affirmatively.

"Well," Clarence Brown adds, "we'll have to take this to the church council. We meet next Tuesday."

"Now on to the preparation of the next year's budget. Who will serve on the stewardship committee for next year?" asks the chairman. His question is followed by dead silence.

Charlie Daly speaks up and says, "I'm concerned that we're raising so much of our money through suppers and bazaars." Joan Seeley answers him by reminding him that it is the sacrificial hard work of people at these events that keeps the church going.

Chairman Brown agrees that money-raising events are important to the church, but he too expresses some fears about the future finances of the church. Finally, he adds, "Well, obviously we're not going to get much done tonight on our new stewardship effort; so I will appoint a committee later, and we'll have a report next time."

A few other minor matters are brought up, such as the need for purchasing light bulbs, getting the fire extinguishers checked, and repairing some leaky faucets. Then the meeting is adjourned.

Evaluation

Clarence Brown knew what he wanted to have happen and did bring an agenda. But, he acted like a loner instead of a leader. He did not get full participation in discussions nor in assuming responsibility. It may not have been all his fault. Perhaps the nominating committee had failed to give him people who were willing to work.

Father Goodrich was strangely silent. Was he intimidated by Mr. Brown?

Why were there not copies of job descriptions of church staff in the hands of the trustees, especially the job description of the custodian?

The theological issue of raising money was cut off by the chairman. Is this why no one would volunteer to serve on the stewardship committee?

Chairman Brown is a hard-working man, but who can help him to learn how to involve other people?

Case Study No. IV—Central Congregational Church

The meeting was called for 7:30 P.M. and the chairman, Mr. Ben Hanson, begins it on time. There are four men present at the beginning, and two others come later. The chairman distributes copies of agendas to all present:

   I. Sanctuary and Educational Building Committee Reports
      1. Painting status
      2. Roof repair status
      3. New business
  II. Grounds Committee
      1. Parking lot and driveway repairs
      2. Signs (no through traffic, no parking, handicapped)
      3. Trash enclosure at Center House
      4. New business
 III. Center House Committee
      1. Roof repairs
      2. Trim repairs
      3. Rental charges
      4. New business

IV. Parsonage Committee
    1. Stove at Associate's house
    2. Painting at Associate's parsonage
    3. New business
V. Report of the Chairman
    1. Meeting with the Finance Committee
    2. Status of insurance
    3. Meeting of the Church Cabinet

The chairman says, "Well, let's get going; the first item will be reported by Jeff, chairman of the Sanctuary and Educational Building Committee."

Jeff informs the group that they are on schedule in regard to painting plans and roofing plans. A roofer has been contracted and will begin next week.

The chairman accepts the report and asks if there are any other needs in the educational building that ought to be mentioned. He gets no reply, and then he remembers the insurance company has sent a letter asking for some response to recommendations they were making.

He goes through the list of recommendations:

    —a new panic bar on the parking-lot door
    —lightning arresters on the educational building
    —taping over the turn-off switch on the fire exit lights (people are snapping them off)
    —new brackets to hang fire extinguishers rather than keep them on the floor
    —orders to remove all combustible materials from the furnace room
    —a need to secure a certificate of liability for the Day Nursery School.

Discussion takes place on each item and each person takes one or more to check out and report back on.

The Grounds Committee chairman reports on the work being done on the parking lot. The company contracted is working too slowly. There is need to pressure them to move faster. One member who knows the company president will make a phone call tonight.

It is pointed out that people are parking on the lawn, because it is closer to the steps, rather than in the parking lot. Signs are needed. The Grounds Committee chairman is overwhelmed with work. Who will help him out? A member volunteers. There will be a sign put up to designate a special place for the handicapped to park.

The trash enclosure has been purchased from the fence company. Now someone is needed to volunteer to pick it up at the lumberyard. One of the members who apparently owns a pick-up truck says he'll get it tomorrow.

The Center House Committee reports, though the chairman is absent tonight. The roof repair is under contract, and one member of the church has volunteered to do the trim painting.

In regard to rental charges at the Center House there seems to be some misunderstanding. Different groups are paying different rates. There is a need for some group to "get it all together." This leads to a discussion of the Center House and who should use it and why.

The member of the Center House Committee has a sheet showing which groups use it and what they pay. A Day Nursery rents two rooms; Weight Watchers rents one room; Parents Without Partners rents one room; and a dancing group rents two rooms. After considerable discussion about how they determine who uses what, they agree that a group should be permitted to rent space only if it completely covers the fixed costs necessary. A subcommittee will be appointed to decide what rates are fair to ask.

The Parsonage Committee reports that the thermostat on the stove in the associate's parsonage is being replaced by one of their members. The other parsonage also needs new trim and wallpapering. The pastor has volunteered to paint and wallpaper the rooms. The trustees agree that if he wants to do this, he can; but if he does not have time, they will find someone to do the work.

New business includes a discussion of insurance coverage. The chairman has a book in front of him that gives all the information about present insurance coverage. They discuss the need of additional liability coverage for special groups in the church like bike-campers who go on hikes from the church each summer. The chairman is authorized to look into increasing coverage.

Evaluation

This was a well-managed and directed board of trustees! The chairman had a clear agenda and knew how to involve all his members.

However, women were noticeably lacking.

Neither of the ministers was present. Perhaps, because they knew the meetings were handled well, they saw no need. However, when it came to a discussion of who uses the Center House, and why, their input and insights would have been very valuable.

There was no prayer, nor did the group ever get to a discussion of the biblical and theological reasons behind the use of the church properties.

The chairman's notebook was a valuable resource item. It was alphabetized with copies of budgets, job descriptions, measurements of buildings and the parking lot, even the measurements of all windows and doors! He was constantly referring to it and could answer questions being raised.

The willingness of members of this board to assume responsibilities indicated a high caliber of leadership and a motivation to run the church in the best way possible.

Questions to Ponder or Discuss

1. Which of the churches described in the case studies had a close working relationship with its treasurer? Which did not?

2. Of the four boards described, which had a few members monopolizing the meeting?

3. Under which of the chairmen cited would you rather serve? Why?

Chapter 9

Trustees Are Ministers, Too

Rachel wondered why Roberto Vera wanted to have lunch with her. She enjoyed being with him; in fact, since she learned to speak Spanish, while in the Peace Corps in Argentina, she hadn't had opportunity to converse with an Hispanic.

"Hola, hermana," Roberto said as he approached the booth with his usual beaming smile.

"Buenas tardes, amigo," responded Rachel, but now she felt uncomfortable about her ability to converse further in his language; so she continued, "I'm mystified, Roberto. You haven't told me why you want to talk with me."

"It's nothing serious," he said, as he seated himself opposite her. "I've got a question I need to answer, and I felt the need of your wisdom."

Rachel felt complimented. Roberto always seemed to say the right thing.

After ordering their lunches and getting the small talk out of the way, Roberto said, "OK, I've kept you in suspense long enough. I wanted to talk with you because I've been asked to serve on the board of trustees."

"Oh-h-h," exclaimed Rachel, "this sounds like a repeat of history." Her mind went back to six years ago when she was first approached to serve on the board. She knew exactly how Roberto felt.

Then she went on to describe to her friend her experience of the previous years and the struggle she had gone through! "But, now I'm in my second term and am vice-chairperson of the trustees. I must say it has been a very fulfilling and meaningful time of service for me."

"Si, pero," began Roberto, and then switching back to English, "I've never done anything like serving on a board of trustees. In my church in San Juan, I was a *diácono* and that's so different."

"That's what I thought. I believed the business type should be a trustee and the spiritual person should be the deacon. However, I've learned otherwise. In fact, I don't think a person should serve on the trustees until he or she has served on some other committee or board."

"Why do you say that?"

"Because when I first joined the trustees, I discovered their priorities and concerns were not the same as mine.

"For example, I'd already served on the missions committee, and at our first meeting as trustees I found them concerned about the interest we were paying on a small loan. Guess what they had done? They had paid that loan off with mission money!"

"But it had already happened, no?" Roberto injected.

"Yes, it had happened but not ever again, while I was on the board. I feel I brought a mission perspective to the others."

"I would like to have the experience with them," Roberto said rather emphatically, "but I would still have to work with finances, investments, and buildings. *No es natural*—for me."

"Roberto, we need you. You're a man of great faith. Even as deacons need faith so do trustees. They run a greater risk in matters of faith because they have to deal with things that are seen."

"I hear what you're saying—'almost, you persuade me.'" Roberto liked to lift Scripture verses out of the Bible and use them in his everyday expressions.

Rachel felt he was now persuaded, but perhaps he needed one more nudge. "Remember the sermon our pastor preached two weeks ago? He said we were all ministers, lay and clergy alike, and he challenged us to break down the wall between 'business things' and 'sacred things.' He called us to respond to the most common tasks with prayer and consecration as a new breed of Christlike people, filled with the Master's spirit and guided by his mind."

"I remember—and I get the message."

Rachel knew another breakthrough had taken place in a life and in her church.

Trusteeship in Christ's Church Is a Ministry

There is a church in Kansas which lists its ministers on the front of the Sunday bulletin, as do most churches. The difference, however, in this church is that above the names of the professional staff it says, "Every member of this church is a minister." Here we have a New Testament reaffirmation of the priesthood of all believers. Each of us who follows and serves the One who said, "I came not to be ministered unto, but to minister" (Matthew 20:28, KJV) must take seriously the ministry of reconciliation and service which has been given as a trust.

Once, when I was talking with a man in Istanbul, Turkey, we each inquired of the other concerning our field of labor. The Turkish gentleman startled me by telling me he was a minister. I responded by informing him that I, too, was a minister. The look on his face told me we were talking about two different kinds of ministers. I discovered he was a minister of the Turkish government, while I was a minister of Christ.

The experience in Istanbul led me to reflect further upon the word "minister." Even as that man was an individual entrusted with a certain aspect of the affairs of state and carrying the authority of the supreme ruler, so I, too (and every other person who carries the name of Christian), am an individual given a trust to carry out under the will of God and the lordship of Jesus Christ.

The discussion between Rachel and Roberto is pertinent for all of us Christians, but even more so to those who have said "yes" to supplying a leadership role in the church. Every member of a board of trustees has been commissioned by the church as Christ's minister to carry on the external affairs of the church but with the approval of the Eternal and the power of the internal Holy Spirit. We are all ministers whether we are caring for the building or reaching for the blind. We are all participants in ministry and mission even in controlling the finances as well as in strengthening the faithful.

The Ministry of Trusteeship Requires a Call and Response

To insist that a member of a board of trustees should have a "divine call" to this task, as much as a professional minister should have a divine call to his or her work, may be frightening and overidealistic for some. It may even be misinterpreted as meaning one should never serve as a trustee unless he or she has some traumatic, cataclysmic Damascus road encounter. This is not my point. What I am saying is that people become trustees because they love God, have known Jesus Christ, and believe they have certain gifts which can enable them to serve effectively. In chapter 1 we noted the ideal "marks of a member of the board of trustees," which we all must attempt to achieve. Now we are adding the call as another underlying dimension of ministry of the board of trustees.

In every call to ministry is the directive "Choose you this day whom ye will serve" (Joshua 24:15, KJV), as given by Joshua to the people of Shechem. In the choice that was set before the people was the exigency of ridding selves of the other gods of materialism, nationalism, and self-centeredness. Every minister of God, whether lay or professional, has to decide whether decisions and actions will be based upon God's Word and way or upon human-kind's.

As I sat with various boards of trustees as an observer, the one thing that surged forth among them was the question "Do we decide this on the basis of the human and secular response, or do we go to the higher Authority?" Oh, no one verbalized it that way, but it was central in conversations and decision making. Those who sensed they had responded as ministers to one another had one way of making decisions, and those who felt they were the final authorities made decisions in the light of that philosophy.

The Ministry of Trusteeship Requires Growth Through Discipline

To be an effective board of trustees' member is to grow through the discipline of prayer. Because most trustees are "business types," too many have surrendered to the idea that to have business skills is to be hard of heart, narrow of mind, and incapable of spiritual growth. Yet each of us has known people with tremendous capabilities in executive and administrative skills who were spiritual giants. Where Christ controls, every talent and skill is transformed into his power. This happens through prayer!

Samuel Johnson was once asked what he felt was the strongest argument for prayer, and he replied, "Sir, there is no argument for prayer." Neither is there a way to browbeat or argue trustees into growth through prayer. This has to be something which comes out of a person's individual walk with God as a minister in service through Christ. It has to come as that quiet, ongoing relationship which seeks the will of the Father in all things. Dr. Harry M. Fosdick, of Riverside Church, New York, used to say, "Prayer is not just resignation, but it is cooperation." This cooperation is with God's people as channels of his will. It is openness to growing beyond where we are to where God would have us be.

A disciplined trustee is one who takes seriously the task entrusted to him or her and, believing it to be a call to ministry, attends every meeting, studies every issue, listens to every opinion, seeks God's will in prayer, and carries through with conviction. That trustee is committed to growing while working.

While studying the Spanish philosopher Miguel de Unamuno in Spain, I learned from his daughter, Maria, that he always wore a special vest he had designed for himself. In one pocket was a New Testament and in the other was a cross. This great thinker and writer was not only the rector and administrator of a large university but also a man who went to his knees with frequency seeking God's will in his business affairs through the teachings of the New Testament and the implications of the cross. No wonder he had such an impact upon his country and the whole Spanish-speaking world. He showed that intellectual discipline and growth, political involvement and growth, and spiritual awareness and growth were all brought together in the Living Word.

The Ministry of Trusteeship Requires Risk and Sacrifice

No one can take up the cross and serve in ministry without running risks. When you serve as a trustee, you will run the risk of being criticized for decisions made, for not doing enough when you hardly have the strength to do more, for being too tight-fisted with the money when the money is all too scarce, and for lacking faith when you have made decisions which require a leap of faith. It is not an easy job.

The work of the trustee is a very time-consuming task. I've known trustees who have given every night of the week, after working all day, to carry out certain jobs at the church.

Sacrifice will be expected and often with very little verbal appreciation. Such is real Christian love and ministry.

Those who handle the finances and investments of the church are often the least commended of people. I've noticed that in churches we ordain deacons and give them certain positions of sitting in honored places in the church; we honor the church school teachers with certificates of recognition; we give the members of the choir a party for their unselfish devotion through the year; but I've never seen a church express appreciation and give honor to the trustees.

The John Wanamaker store in Philadelphia during the Lenten season has displayed Michael Munkácsy's marvelous painting of the crucifixion. If you examine it closely, as I have during a visit to that city, you will see a man in the foreground of the painting who appears to be about to run away from the cross. But something seems to halt him in his tracks. He is half turned toward the cross.

Even as this man who is setting out toward the center of activity has his gaze fixed on the cross, so we who are trustees of the church need to keep our eyes fixed on that cross. We love because He loved us. He ministered with sacrifice of body and soul; so must we.

The Ministry of Trusteeship Requires the Larger Vision

Even as deacons and elders must have a vision which comes from God regarding the direction and growth of the church, so too must the trustees be sharers of that vision. "Where there is no vision, the people perish" (Proverbs 29:18, KJV).

There are some key teachings for us concerning the

visionary aspects of our ministry as trustees in the Gospel account of Jesus' temptation in Matthew 4:1-11.

The struggle of Jesus in the wilderness was caused by his having been commissioned to a task which was from above. His temptation is also that of those who have been given a task within the church. In verses 3-4 the devil says, "If you are the Son of God, command these stones to become loaves of bread." This was a personal challenge of Jesus' power. Should he presume on his power? This is a question which each of his followers is asked when one has been given certain power within the church. Even a trustee is tempted to use power incorrectly.

The second phase of his temptation came when the Lord was led up to a high place and invited to jump proving nothing would happen to destroy him (vv. 5-6). This was the temptation to be spectacular, or sensational. How many of us are tempted to the superficially spectacular or sensational in order to boost our own egos before others rather than do God's will?

The third aspect of Jesus' temptation was to be offered the kingdoms of the world if he would but yield his power to the evil forces. Here we see the crux of political corruptive power; just compromise and give in to the expediencies of the hour! (See verses 8-9.) Those given the power over buildings, money, and systems are subject to the same temptations. We are offered our own little kingdom within the local church where we can wield power with a fury. More than one church has been disrupted or divided because some trustees yielded to the misuse of power.

In this epic of temptation our Lord proved himself by

turning aside the evil pull in affirming three counter-facts:

1. "Man shall not live by bread alone, but by every word that proceeds from the mouth of God" (4:4, RSV). Here Jesus asserts he will not do anything just to satisfy his own desire.

2. "Again it is written, 'You shall not tempt the Lord, your God'" (4:7, RSV). Here Jesus says he will not misuse the power given him.

3. "You shall worship the Lord your God, and him only shall you serve" (4:10, RSV). Here Jesus was saying what he said in Gethsemane, "Not my will but thine."

The larger vision of every trustee should be based upon the Word of God and the direction sought in prayer. The larger vision must be seen as the need of the larger church and the larger will. As a trustee I must never let my limited view become blurred by my own power. And finally, the larger vision is always looking at all aspects of God's church and world with the prayer on my lips, "Not my will but thine be done."

I have been to Jerusalem twice, and each time I visited all the places so sacred to Christians. Perhaps the place which meant most to me was the hill of Golgotha (Gordon's) outside the ancient city walls. To be sure, no one is certain whether or not this is where Christ was crucified. There is much archaeological evidence that criminals were put to death on this strange hill which still looks like a human skull.

As I stood on an opposite hill looking at what might be the place where Jesus was put to death, I was impressed by what I saw. First, there was the ancient wall of Jerusalem which had risen and fallen so many times according to the warring madness of men. Then, there was a marketplace and a bus station just outside the wall.

Did our Lord hang on that cross and look down at the marketplace where the business people were too busy even to note his agony-filled love? Did Jesus look at that old wall and remember how the followers of God had built it as the sacred city where the Father would be worshiped, and did his heart break because they had forgotten the Creator and Redeemer, as they misused their power for personal aggrandizement?

Whatever our Lord thought as he hung there, my thoughts were on his vision. He had turned it over to me and to other members of his church.

The trustees of the church are the enablers of the fulfillment of his vision. As his ministers we are called to become his voice, eyes, ears, hands, and feet in the world he loved so much.

Questions to Ponder or Discuss

1. What do you think a "call to minister" implies for lay people?
2. What are some specific risks you might take in serving as a trustee in your church?
3. What were the three temptations of Jesus and how do they apply to boards of trustees?

Appendixes

Appendix A

Maintenance Checklist
for Church Buildings

Who does checking?	Best time for checking	Things to be checked out
(example) Mildred Broten	Spring	**Church Sanctuary**—Are pews clean? Is organ functioning well? Have floors been cleaned? Is pulpit lighting effective? Are windows tight and workable? Do walls need painting? Is heating adequate?
Andrew Simmons	Winter	**Church Kitchen**—Has it been cleaned regularly? Are faucets tight? Check drains? Do refrigerator and stove need cleaning? Have inventory of silverware and dishes.

Who does checking?	Best time for checking	Things to be checked out
Joe Kallard	Fall	**Furnace Room**—Has furnace had annual cleaning and adjusting? Same with air conditioning? Are fire regulations being observed? Check chimney and mechanisms.
Andrew Simmons	Every Month	**Toilets and Washrooms**—Are they bright and clean? Properly supplied with towels and tissues? Are toilet bowls clean? Is there a need for painting or improving? Does all plumbing function properly?
Mildred Broten	Every Month	**Church Office and Pastor's Study**—Are they cleaned regularly? Is the staff content? Has there been spring washing of windows? Do windows work well? Is there a need for painting? Are office supplies properly stored?
Bill Holten	Spring and Fall	**Church Grounds**—Check sidewalks, ramps, and stairs. Is there a need for repairs? Care for lawn—fertilize and seed when necessary. Check church signs for need of painting or repairs. Trim shrubs and trees. Make certain parking lot is clear and properly marked. Check outside lighting.

Who does checking?	Best time for checking	Things to be checked out
Bill Holten	Spring and Fall	**Church Buildings—Exterior—**Is there a need for painting wood or pointing the bricks? Check roof—downspouts and gutters. Do they need to be replaced or redirected? Remove leaves from gutters. Check effects of ice or snow.
Joan Thackery	Every Month	**Christian Education Building—**Make certain there is weekly dusting and cleaning. Wash twice a year. Check furniture for needed repairs or painting. Tune pianos once a year (or as required by weather). Check with Church School Superintendent regarding needs for supplies. Check ceilings and walls for needed repairs or painting. Check lighting to be sure it is adequate and cheerful.

Appendix B

Energy Conservation

1. Gather all available data on energy use patterns for the last five years. (If possible, have someone diagram the various types of energy flow for each section of the building by program use and convert all values to a common unit such as BTU's.)

2. Analyze the thermal characteristics of the building:
   a. Identify air infiltration factors related to "tightness" of the building
   b. Determine conduction losses through exterior surfaces based on the relationship between thermal resistance (R Factor) in ceilings, walls and floors and "degree" days for the area
   c. Consider the impact of factors in the natural environment such as sun, wind, earth and vegetation

3. Some assumptions in determining life cycle costing:
   a. Energy costs will go up a rate of 8-10% a year
   b. Most churches will have to borrow to make improvements, so interest charges must be included in the total cost
   c. Some improvements will require significant future maintenance which should be included in the total cost

4. Some practical action possibilities:
   a. Seal all cracks around windows, doors, and other

places where air leaks occur, and install storm windows and doors

b. Install carpet and thermal padding on all tile and similar floors (warmer floors may permit lowering of thermostat settings)

c. Insulate all ceilings to reflect a payback period of not more than 10 years (consider the options of placing the insulation on either the interior or exterior of the roof and compare costs and benefits of both options with probable need for future roof replacement and possible installation of solar collection system)

d. Modify entrances, particularly on the north and west, to include double doors with air locks

e. Install rigid insulation on the exterior of all appropriately exposed exterior walls (a masonry finish can be applied which is similar to stucco in appearance) and panels of insulation on interior walls where it is desirable to retain exterior brick or other appearances

f. Determine major wind direction during winter and use plantings, earth berms and wind shields to divert prevailing winds during cold weather

g. Consider the feasibility of installing an active solar heating system, using the south-facing roof area for solar collectors and demonstrating a payback period of not more than 20 years.

Appendix C[1]

Dear Pastor:

The latest National Fire Protection Association statistics show over 4,000 church fires have occurred during the past year with a dollar loss of $26,500,000. We feel very fortunate that our city had a near perfect record with little fire loss in church buildings. Perhaps a better word to describe our situation would be lucky. We do have the potential for loss, and we realize fire prevention is a never-ending responsibility.

Therefore, we are asking every pastor in the city to make a special effort to promote fire prevention in his church. This might be accomplished by assigning someone from the board of trustees to this job or, if possible, to assume the job personally. We will appreciate your assistance. The following guidelines may be useful to you in evaluating your building:

1. **Exit Requirements** Exit Corridors—Stairs—Doors—Foyers are required means of egress and must be kept clear of obstructions of any kind.

Exit Doors must be maintained operable from the inside without any special knowledge, and must be equipped with the following type of hardware: A. For under 100-occupant load, freewheeling hardware is approved. B. For over 100-occupant load, panic hardware must be provided (exception—the main entrance may be equipped with a dead bolt key lock provided there is a readily visible metallic sign

[1] *ABEC Gram* (Valley Forge, Pa.), vol. 4, no. 1 (Spring, 1978), pp. 5, 8, 10.

adjacent to the doorway which reads "This door must remain unlocked during occupancy.")

Unapproved locks—Do not install dead-boltslide or thumb bolt, chains, or any other unapproved locking device on an exit door. Check if you are not sure.

2. **Boiler and Furnace Rooms** Storage of any kind is prohibited in furnace or boiler rooms. Doors to these areas are to be kept closed. Keep fresh air windows, louvers, etc., free of obstructions.

3. **Interior Finish of Wall and Ceiling Materials** All materials used during construction of building must meet certain criteria. Do not apply paneling, ceiling tile, etc., without checking with your church fire inspector.

4. **Draperies—Curtains—Decorations** Materials used for these purposes are required to meet certain criteria. Materials (other than fiberglass) must be treated periodically every five to seven years, or after cleaning, with a flame-retardant solution. This treatment can be done commercially, or by members of the church, using the following solutions which can be applied by dipping or spraying: 9 ounces of Borax, 4 ounces of Boric Acid, mixed in one gallon of water. Plastics cannot be treated and should not be used for this purpose. Other decorations such as straw, hay, trees (especially Christmas trees), boughs, and wall hangings must be treated with a fire retardant. A solution that can be applied to evergreens, etc., can be made by mixing one pound of ammonium sulfate (fertilizer grade) with 1¼ pints of water for each 4 feet of tree. Other materials should be saturated.

5. **Storage of Gasoline and/or Powered Equipment** Lawn

mowers, tractors, edgers, etc., are not permitted to be stored inside the building—gasoline storage is prohibited.

6. **Flammable and Combustible Liquids** These materials in the form of paint, oil thinner, duplicating fluid, etc., may be stored in the building, provided they are kept in a closed metal cabinet located in an approved storage room or area.

7. **Fire Extinguishers** All extinguishers are required to be kept operable and should be recharged after any use. They must be serviced annually by a qualified person or agency.

8. **Automatic Fire Extinguishing Systems** All commercial sized kitchen ranges are required to be equipped with an automatic fire extinguishing system (CO_2 or dry chemical), installed in the hood and duct system. This system, when activated, is also designed to shut off fuel and exhaust fan. NOTE: Domestic (home type) ranges are not required to have this system.

9. **Occupancy Limits of Rooms and Areas** In areas of fixed seating such as in the sanctuary or chapel, the occupant load is determined at the time of installation—all other areas and rooms 15 square feet per person. Overloading of facilities presents an undue hazard which cannot be permitted. Signs are available for posting of occupant loads by requesting them from the Fire Prevention office.

10. **Use of Candles** Candles may be used, providing they are set in well-anchored, noncombustible holders and away from combustible materials: On tables, candles must be in noncombustible holders and be provided with glass globes; In candelabrums, securely supported; In enclosed (globes) processional staffs or standards. NOTE: Hand-held candles are not permitted except to light tapers in candelabrums

during ceremonies. These are not to be carried down aisles or held by persons in pews or choir lofts.

11. **Construction and/or Remodeling** Permits must be obtained through the Central Inspection Division for any change in structure or for installing of wall or ceiling material.

12. **Trash Storage** Trash containers (wastebaskets) should be emptied daily into trash storage containers which are of a closed metal type.

13. **Housekeeping** Storage areas should be kept in a well ordered manner and periodic attention should be given to the elimination of unused or not needed combustibles that can be disposed of. Good housekeeping is essential for fire prevention.

14. **Closing Checks** A good policy for any building is to appoint a responsible person to make a check of appliances and heating devices prior to closing the building at night and after services.

15. **Electric Wiring/Panels** Electrical wiring must be done by a licensed electrician after obtaining a permit through the Central Inspection Division at the City Building. Extension cord wiring is permitted for temporary use *only* and is not to be used as a permanent fixture. Cords on appliances and machines are required to plug directly into receptacles within the length of their cords (usually 6—8 ft.), without splices. Electric panels are to be kept clear of storage and should be marked to indicate area of control.

16 **Gas-Fired Heating or Cooking Devices** Installation must be done by a licensed installer and a permit obtained through the Central Inspection Division.

17. **Carpeting** There are no restrictions on the type of carpeting you may install in your church, except carpet with extremely long nap or one that is proven to be highly combustible would not be approved. However, if your church has any intention of providing a child day care center now or in the future, it would be wise to purchase carpet that will meet the requirements of child care licensing regulations (i.e., 0-76 in all categories flame rate spread, fuel contributed and smoke developed) and obtain a letter of certification from the supplier which states this information.

18. **Basements—Balconies** Basements used for any purpose other than service of the building (i.e., furnace, boiler, electrical, refrigeration equipment) shall be provided with two approved means of egress, one of which must go directly to the outside at ground level. (Windows are not considered as exits.) Balconies with an occupant load of over ten (10) persons are required to have two approved exits. For ten (10) or under a capacity sign (available from the Fire Prevention office) shall be posted. Each level of the building shall be provided with two approved means of egress (exception, see balcony requirements).

Respectfully,
THE WICHITA FIRE DEPARTMENT